Steven

It is inspiring to meet
business leaders who place values
attraction over transactional fee-taking!
Thor achieved an important standard in
entrepreneurism. May you never lose touch
with what makes your organization worth
admiring. Maybe all corporate head quarters
should be confined to a bungalow and
their leaders prefer a pub over fine dining;

With respect.

[signature]
[signature]

THE NATURE OF CHAOS
IN BUSINESS

THE NATURE OF CHAOS IN BUSINESS

IN BUSINESS

USING COMPLEXITY TO FOSTER SUCCESSFUL ALLIANCES AND ACQUISITIONS

J. GARRETT RALLS, JR.
WITH
KIMBERLY A. WEBB

Cashman Dudley
An imprint of Gulf Publishing Company
Houston, Texas

THE JUNE RUSCHE HAMRAH
CAMP FOR ALL

A portion of this book's royalties goes to the Camp For All
Foundation (Houston, Texas; ph. 713-686-5666), which
sponsors a barrier-free camp created to provide unique camping
and retreat experiences for children and adults with special needs.

THE NATURE OF CHAOS
IN BUSINESS

Cashman Dudley
An imprint of Gulf Publishing Company
P.O. Box 2608 ☐ Houston, Texas 77252-2608

10 9 8 7 6 5 4 3 2 1

Library of Congress Cataloging-in-Publication Data

Ralls, J. Garrett, Jr.
   The nature of chaos in business : using complexity to foster
successful global alliances / J. Garrett Ralls, Jr. with Kimberly
A. Webb.
      p.   cm.
   Includes bibliographical references and index.
   ISBN 0-88415-504-8 (alk. paper)
   1. Strategic alliances (Business) 2. Chaotic behavior
in systems. 3. Management.   I. Webb, Kimberly A.
II. Title.
HD69. S8R35   1999
658'.044—DC21   99-20622
                                                            CIP

Printed in the United States of America.
Printed on acid-free paper (∞).

iv

Contents

Preface

This book is about relationships in business. Our vantage point is the beginning of an important transition for our global economy in which alliances must be more than a good idea. They must work in order for many of us to succeed in our careers and as investors.

Most alliances fail altogether or yield only partial success. Many businesspeople see alliances as a necessary compromise. They prefer to go it alone if possible. A global economy, networked by electronic communication and often pursuing complicated technologies, requires alliances to perform at its best.

To succeed at alliances and other strategic business relationships, we must acquire new knowledge of what the marketplace is. Our view of the business landscape must be broad, track the dynamism among the many elements, and be understood for its inherent opportunity. Denial and other avoidance of change are no longer options.

OUR SWARM

Our premises in this book are grounded in the realities of our clients and tenets of global business leaders and futurists.

Much like a swarm of bees in flight, events around the world hover together and are closely linked by instantaneous communication and interdependent economies. Today the world's population is nearly 6 billion. At the midpoint of the 20th century, we were only 2.5 billion. With the world's population expanding and getting denser, the meaning of personal space at home and work has changed. This growing density does not end here. Advancing communication technology creates a virtual human density with e-mailing, inexpensive telephone calling, and worldwide paging. As expected, the nature of relationships in any aspect of business means something different from what it meant last year or last week. Relationships between you and your customers, as well as among your partners in the value chain, largely determine your enterprise's wealth.

The swarm across the business landscape reveals that business relations are at risk to the disorder of chaos. Nonetheless, the same phenomenon presents us with a hive of new opportunity. To create and mine the honey, we must possess new knowledge of how to work together, manage the turbulence, and grasp the emerging pathways to success.

As we later explain, the Santa Fe Institute is an interdisciplinary group of gifted researchers. They focus on complexity at any level of life—microscopic viruses, the human body, sociology, and economics. With other complexity theorists, Santa Fe Institute researchers are bringing a new view of our world to us with an important vocabulary.

The vocabulary is based on life, is simple to understand, and is able to be shared across professions and skills. It constitutes a language to combine life-based views of organizations. The new vocabulary broadens participation beyond the audience of change practitioners, a few well-informed clients, and academicians. Eventually it may invite the world to a common understanding that humankind in organizations is more like the workings of the human body than a mechanical process of control and efficiency. Though many have a vocabulary of change, it is often shallow and rarely represents genuine values. Too often words are created to mask intent or are overused with "no walk to the talk." In either case, the words obscure meaningful change.

Our contribution to the new understanding is to focus on the workings of a firm and on business relationships between firms and their customers. We examine the intricacies of trust, communication, and creative tensions that bind strategic business relations and prompt creativity. Our quest is to reveal how your personal choices in concert with others' can blend enduring value with a life worth living.

"Swarms" are the rage in the talk of high techies and Internet junkies. Like "e-mail," "web," and "chat room," "swarm" is destined to be a part of our vocabulary. A swarm is the interconnection of many dumb chips in cyberspace with an intelligent processor. The processor creates new knowledge from the swarm's inputs. As Kevin Kelly, editor of *Wired* magazine, writes, "We see the same dynamic at work in other domains: Dumb cells in our body work together in a swarm to produce an incredibly smart immune system. . . . Dumb parts, properly connected into a swarm, yield smart results."*

Our book is the product of two career swarms. An array of human events, when connected together, offers insight to our ever-turbulent business world. What makes up our swarm is experience in strategic business relationships across industries and around the world. Each experience is rich in understanding. Interconnected, they create a knowledge in personal and business relations for capturing value and personal satisfaction in the "new economy" Kevin Kelly describes.

CREDIT WITHOUT LIABILITY

We credit our mentors and clients as the catalysts for our knowledge. They deserve recognition for the insight you may gain from this book. The responsibility for missed opportunities or mistakes is ours. We regret there are many who deserve recognition who are not stated by name in what follows. Our aspiration is to describe the swarm of personalities, paradigms, and events that comprise this book.

Client requests are the impetus behind this book. While our clients valued the insights from our presentations, they wanted a book they could review so they could apply their new knowledge in varied circumstances.

A big part of the book came from coaching discussions and debates between the two of us. Kimberly has worked with me since she was in college. The mentoring discussions between us proved to accelerate her growth. Kimberly suggested that we add the war stories and discussions to the book to guide others entering the business world. As we traveled the world on consulting assignments, Kimberly recorded in her journal what advice and guidance served her best. As is the case for most mentors, I learned from her challenges and crisp insights.

---

* Kelly, Kevin. *New Rules for the New Economy: 10 Radical Strategies for a Connected World,* New York: Viking, 1998, p. 13.

THE FLIGHT OF OUR SWARM
INTO TODAY'S CHAOS

Chaos theory gained in popularity in recent years as a way to decode the mystery of the universe and nature. Enthralled in controversy for some as a challenge to creationism, the body of knowledge neither proves nor disproves the claims of theology for us. What it does do is bring forth a life-based view of the world.

By "life-based view" we mean that we use metaphors of life itself to describe how people make personal and business choices. We think in terms of interconnected parts just as our organs, skeleton, skin, neural systems, blood, chemistry and the like constitute our bodies. In other words, a change in one organ may affect another. Our thoughts can be functions of past and present experiences at the same time.

So we must determine how one part of a system influences the rest. In this manner, we can view trends, capture emerging opportunities, set patterns for growth, and optimize our use of resources across the entire system. This is true of any system, an economy, the way a firm is organized, how we manage our careers, or how our bodies' immune system works.

A life-based view is a more accurate portrayal of what happens among people than linear models derived from the logic of technology. We are released more and more from the constraints of this viewpoint as technology itself becomes more lifelike. Biotechnology is a function of life itself. Information technology and telecommunication are talked about as networks. These networks behave in dynamic ways more akin to life itself. They supplant the linearity in mechanical switches and electrical wires or build swarms where dumb chips create intelligence. These networks underlie all industries and thus emerge to transform all technology into dynamic, lifelike models.

NO LONGER A STRAIGHT LINE

From chaos theory, complexity theory springs forth. It examines the nature of what happens at the edge of chaos, a place where most business decisions are made. Complexity theorists point to a major shift in our view of the world. Technology no longer drives our view of the world. Traditionally, the derivative fields for mathematics and logic—i.e., law, accounting, and engineering—have reinforced humankind's view of the world that things are logical.

Mechanical power is a logical or linear progression based on what we see being done in a manufacturing process. We expect life to follow a like progression of events. We see inputs gathered on which work is done to produce outputs; in turn these are channeled to customers. The parallel mechanical view of humans is that we see, think, and then react. The reality, however, is very different. We are always perceiving things, even while we act. We are always thinking, guiding our every move as we act, and accommodating each new perception or sensation.

In business we set a strategy, and it must persevere through the ever-growing chaos. Not so long ago, we were taught that if we envision an opportunity in the market, make an offering, promote and support the offering, then we will earn a profit. Unfortunately, life is not so simple. We were so focused on the linear, we ignored the reality of the craziness that shaped business reality, diminished opportunity, or excessively consumed resources.

Reality in offerings today must be more responsive to customers and a global market. This necessitates more interaction and greater precision with the flexibility to adapt to constant change. These requirements make business life increasingly complex.

Complexity is compounded by the need to win the acceptance of a strategy by a work force and myriad partners in the value chain. A value chain is the business relationship that exists from suppliers to vendors to providers of services or products to end users. Complicated technologies and global market channels require numerous parties to complete value chains. At every junction, there are chances for distraction and disorder. Adding to the complexity, acceptance for a business initiative must address the understanding, preferences, and views of employees, customers, and partners and how what happens impacts their lives and powers to act. Efforts to communicate, persuade, and educate must often cross cultural and language barriers, as well as accommodate varying degrees of experience, skill, and knowledge.

The complexity is a Gordian knot no sword of a modern Alexander-like executive can cut to access value. The value chain functions best when the linkages are sustained or strengthened over time. Strategic business relations are the key to making money as the complexity accelerates in the marketplace.

With complexity you cannot easily extrapolate past events into a straight line and predict the future. When business—financial, manufacturing, sales, and services—focused on the growing domestic market in the post-World War II prosperity, linear forecasts offered precision sufficient to add value. Now linear forecasting has extended beyond its usefulness and into our era. Today, a host of influences competes against you while you juggle dozens of value components to make things happen. Issues and influences are scattered across a landscape of value.

It is a misnomer to speak of "value chains." This implies a simple, linear process. Value networks, in reality, web together myriad possibilities. You can seek value from any direction and pursue value across many pathways. You outsource your advertising to a Madison Avenue firm, taking a senior partner of the firm on as a part-time vice-president of advertising. You may have your primary code programmed in India and your product manufactured in Malaysia, while product development and marketing are done in Texas. Financing may come from a local bank branch of a New York financial institution with backing from U.S. and European pension funds. Your customers may be anywhere. Such is the dispersion of value components and links in our world. Such is the nature of complexity as it impacts our business.

THE ROAD TO SANTA FE

The Santa Fe Institute (SFI) is an interdisciplinary cadre that is advancing the understanding of complexity in business. We have attended their recent annual business meetings at the invitation of Susan Ballati, director, and Ellen Goldberg, president. How we learned of them and earned the invitations illustrate how networks function to spread knowledge and its value.

Kimberly began working with me while she was in her last years as an undergraduate. With fellow student workers, she ran the firm's beach house conference center. Our first conversation about chaos was to pursue computer printouts of a chaos math model for her Unix and C programming course. The calculus and scattergrams meant little to me. I had read about chaos theory and watched it unfold as an interest among my scientific clients. Their interest meant little or nothing to Kimberly, and that day's conversation turned to the supply of oatmeal cookies for the next group of clients.

A year or so later, a lecture series for the Defense Advanced Research Project Agency (DARPA) on partnering in dual-use technology led to an invitation to the National Defense Center in Hawaii to address the same topic. Here we met key staff from the Office of Naval Research (ONR) and became involved in an effort to accelerate commercialization of a Navy lab technology.

At ONR we learned about the Santa Fe Institute. George Keller, a retired Air Force officer, was on contract to a beltway bandit think tank serving ONR and other defense intelligence community agencies. George is a brilliant eclectic, always in search of a better way. A willing mentor, George shared the conceptual view of complexity presented in this book.

Revealed here is a series of shared interests, networked across associated but often competing organizations. Different from the past, these entities vigorously shared ideas and resources despite their competitiveness . . . the new rules Kevin Kelly writes about.

George's insight stirred our curiosity, and we began to investigate SFI and readings by its researchers. We discovered their insights that express in everyday terms how life in business, or any aspect of our lives, goes about shaping choices for humankind. We have long valued this organic, systemic view. At SFI, we found more disciplines sharing a language and offering further insights.

We learned everything we could about SFI from many sources. Coincidentally, a couple of years earlier a colleague, Ed Allday, thought of using SFI as a meeting site but passed on it. The think-tank-styled environment did not lend itself to our objectives. We called to gain Ed's views on SFI again. Readied with his positive report and new knowledge of chaos and complexity, we made first contact.

We complimented SFI and pledged to enlighten our network as to SFI's mission. Our curiosity and earnest offer to sponsor SFI to our network was greeted with the gracious invitation to visit. The opportunity to listen firsthand to these researchers inspired us to incorporate complexity views into this book. After witnessing a leading fund manager's endorsement of complexity theory and crediting it as a basis for his outstanding year-in, year-out performance, we knew there had to be value in it. The premises for the U.S. Department of Justice's challenge of Microsoft evolved from Brian Arthur's work at SFI. This application of chaos theory further convinced us of the value of the complexity viewpoint.

Most persuasive was a conference paper on a new means of evading cyber intrusion based upon the human immune system. The system was a product of a cyber expert carpooling with a microbiologist. They taught one another their professional niche vocabularies and models. The cross-disciplinary solution emerged from the common ground and seeing life dynamics at work in cyber space.

Perched on the side of a hill with a breathtaking vista of New Mexico, SFI recently dedicated its new "cave and commons" addition to its facility. Like its faculty, who come from research, academic, and business institutions around the world, the "cave and commons" structure was borrowed from another place—MIT. SFI is a place where what is best is pursued first—above jealousies and turf disputes. Still a human organization, it has imperfections. Consistent yet again with the complexity view, SFI leverages imperfections to spawn creativity and advance innovation. To these good people, we express profound appreciation for inspirations reflected in this book. Any errors are our own. We credit the people of SFI with great insight for the good of humanity.

APPRECIATION TO MENTORS

Valuing the work of SFI researchers takes preparation. A systems view often needs nurturing because it is often counter to established scientific rigor. For example, Brian Arthur, whose work is explored in this book, for years faced resistance to his views on complexity in the field of economics.

The systemic view is complicated and at times difficult in its proof. The linear view is easier to digest. So much attention has been given linear, empirical views, we benchmark without thinking; we peg ourselves to someone else's history while he proceeds to the future.

We have built on the discoveries of a variety of systemic thinkers. They saw and described organizations as organisms—dynamic and alive; capable of great fun, excitement, and value.

I (Ralls) was first mentored in the organic view by Clay Aldefer, then at Yale University and later when he worked with me on a project for the U.S. government. Clay introduced me to the A. K. Rice Institute and Washington School of Psychiatry's Tavistock Learning Symposia. There, craziness was genuinely simulated for a lasting understanding of dynamism in groups and firms. Later, my first boss at Exxon, the late Bob Nemecek, taught me how to use a dynamic view of the world to judge the stock market. Carolyn Lukensmeyer and Herb Shepard of the Cleveland Gestalt Institute mentored me in several projects at Exxon. With Barry Macy of The Texas Center for Productivity and the Quality of Work Life, Carolyn and Herb guided large-scale organization change efforts under my leadership. They built on the boundary notions that Alderfer introduced me to and strengthened my ability to move client group dynamics. Don Chase of Innovation Associates taught me about creative tension and nonlinear thinking and their value to innovation.

Warren Nielson taught me to tell war stories to convey meaning and to bring others' experiences alive for the benefit of learning without living it. Warren also taught me the value of realistic, simple simulations.

They all taught me what I teach clients: Do not expect things to be rational in business. There are too many expectations colliding. Set a focus through the craziness. Watch for changes. Be persistent, yet adapt as needed.

James Yunker, author of *How to Make Corporate Marriages Work* in the 1970s and veteran of ITT's go-go days of mergers and later GTE's acquisitions, taught me how to demystify integrating organizations. His practical views are still valuable guidelines. James addressed the craziness of mergers with transparency and straight talk.

Finally, we must credit on-going relationships for expanding our view of the international business landscape. These added to our first-hand global view. I benefited over the years from participating in the Asia Society and the Society of International Business Fellows. We both benefited from David Young's Oxford Analytica (OA) Annual International Business Conference.

In describing the craziness in firms, I like to tell this war story as a reminder:

The setting was a meeting between Bill Paul, then Exxon Chemicals' senior change consultant, and me, shortly after I arrived at Exxon from my government job. Bill asked me how my job was going. I said I found Exxon to be a smooth, rational operation compared to the craziness of the U.S. government. I confessed to being perplexed by the fact that people in both places, the government and Exxon, said their workplace was crazy and completely irrational. Same words, different places. Bill commented that sanity was often a function of where you had just been.

ATTENTION TO THE CUSTOMER

The lion's share of credit for this book goes to our clients. Had they not shared their career and business experiences, we would have no validation but our own limited views for the insights offered by SFI and our mentors.

Kevin Kelly claims that in our Internet and networked world, there is one precious thing, "The only factor becoming scarce in a world of abundance is human attention." He goes on to quote Nobel Prize winner Herbert Simon, "What information consumes . . . is the attention of its recipients. Hence a wealth of information creates a poverty of attention."*

We too see attention as scarce. It is difficult to get people to alter their patterns or take the time to reflect and choose patterns of greater consequence to their businesses and lives. Customer intimacy suffers as people find it easier to stay where they are than learn from a customer what might require change or otherwise upset the applecart.

Attention is abused. The media shower under which we all live can be manipulated. Repeating half-truths can turn them into reality in the minds of voters. Overexposure deadens our attention. Stretching things out over time hastens indifference. Politicians in our nation and in the marketplace know these tactics well.

Our intent is to honor the reader's attention with realistic tenets for building business relationships. In this book, we have given our clients attention from two views: meeting them where they are now and seeing them as they can be. To this end, the book unveils pathways to a future some clients have yet to envision. Our clients have taught us a great deal. We hope the book strengthens visions for what can be.

MESSAGE TO MENTORS AND CLIENTS

A final note to our mentors and clients: Implied in the learnings we took from you is a hope for life worth living at work. This concept of a life worth living embodies for us material success and personal fulfillment.

---

* *Ibid*, p. 59.

Another learning from Kevin Kelly is, "In the past, an innovation's momentum indicated significance. Now, in the network environment, where biological behavior reigns, significance precedes momentum."* The recent efforts of firms to transform themselves in terms of trust, flexibility, adaptation, and openness leave us hopeful.

The significance we have long sought may be in the willingness to address business for what it is, a collection of firms that are a collection of people who are biological organisms—crazy, dynamic, and creative. The factor needed for us to realize a life worth living on a broad scale may just be this understanding. The intent of this book is to bridge the reality of today with the old promise of a better tomorrow. Our odds are getting better.

J. Garrett Ralls, Jr.
Kimberly A. Webb
Bentwater on the Lake, Texas

---

* *Ibid*, p. 35.

INTRODUCTION

Chaos in Alliances and Acquisitions

The pursuit of value now and in the future is turbulent, every day advancing in complexity. The insight to adapt within chaos, and join with others, determines market performance. Complicated alliances, joint ventures, mergers, and value chain partnerships lay pipelines across the business landscape for economic value. Value readily flows through the pipelines as a focus on emerging growth strategies penetrates the chaos.

In the twenty-first century, grasping order from chaos will be the source of business acumen. Complexity is the point where order meets chaos. At this junction, precision and relationships are paramount. A company needs precision to create economic openings. Relationships are necessary for projecting pathways to the openings.

In chaos, there are two ways to access economic value. One is to emerge with patterns which create a new order for business. As patterns repeat across a business landscape, they begin to dominate. This is known as the principle of increasing returns in chaos. Whether by intention or adaptation, for good or bad, patterns evolve to a new order. When shaped to create value, patterns are powerful economic tools.

Optimization, that is, making systems, processes, or procedures as efficient, cost-effective, and productive as possible, is the other means for accessing value. Today's businesses consolidate, reengineer, or transform to optimize against diminishing returns, even if improvement is minimal or incremental. In sharp contrast, setting patterns for increasing returns offers new growth with unlimited potential.

Soon everyone in the world will have access to value through capitalism. Capitalism, however, cannot be unfettered. A sustainable environment warrants restraint for how we conduct business and govern in order to ensure human survival. Increasing population, migration to commercial centers, and the resulting density in urban areas, for example, force the adaptation of revenue-generating technology to nature's demands as a life necessity. Business processes such as product manufacturing must exist within the tolerances of air and water. This complication begs for attention and invites participation from across the community.

In the present complexity of global economic growth, a life worth living—at home and work—is expected but elusive. Myriad expectations must be managed among diverse and numerous individuals, firms, communities, markets, and societies. To capture the opportunity in the ensuing complexity, a new era of management must emerge to create value through strategic business relations.

Firms in the twenty-first century will emit catalysts which bond them to other enterprises. Partnering with resources, talent, and knowledge will better enable the intersection of forces which create commercial opportunities. Combining capabilities enhances:

- Access to new markets
- The bundling of old and new technologies to create still other product innovations
- The ability to attract capital
- Leverage in the use of infrastructures

Effective relations with communities and governments will heighten sensitivity for social responsibility and changing policy. Strategic business relations will establish and maintain pipelines for value creation.

Unlike the predominant twentieth century experience, companies cannot permit partnerships in the future to unwind, fail in mission, or stumble along with mediocre performance. The interlocking of firms will actually gain in importance for business growth, global strategies, and rapid technology improvement. Twenty-first century business leaders will need to take greater care in choosing partners, sequencing relationships, adding value, negotiating, planning joint business, managing commitments, deploying capital, sharing operations and stewardship, resolving conflicts or disputes, and implementing growth or exit strategies.

The twentieth century continues to yield marvelous advancements and create tremendous wealth. At times the opportunity cost, or trade-off, was excessive in terms of exploitation of nature, constraints to personal fulfillment, and unrealized dreams for creating wealth. Nonetheless, in this century, humankind evolved from the industrial era and established increasingly optimal business systems.

Revitalizing work systems is a form of growth ignored or put in the spotlight for only the period of initiation. Vitality in firms and their partnerships is like human vitality, requiring daily exercise and care.

The information technology of the last half century advanced efficacy by optimizing against the economic and physical laws of diminishing returns. Companies now have a wide range of information technology and microbiology to call on, from Taylor's "scientific management" to operations research to reengineering, eliminating waste, cost containment, and others that will make business operations more efficient. Empowerment and teamwork practices invite meaningful involvement in business and high performance outcomes, yet, with all their accomplishments, these methods have become more commodities than management tools.

Everyone is using them, so their effectiveness is reduced as a competitive advantage as they are widely applied as "best practices." Any method for optimizing eventually suffers its own deminishing returns. Variances in application exist but blur over time. What constitutes "optimal" in mechanical, linear systems is unclear in the chaos of globalization. Frustration echoes across industries as managers realize the limitations of optimization.

What's next is understanding the complexity in the business landscape, the totality of factors that create your market, competition, distribution system, supply of raw materials, and other aspects of your business environment. Companies are not abandoning optimization. They are subordinating it to agendas for adapting to market forces and emerging strategies. As firms stand at the edge of chaos in the twenty-first century, they embellish value by setting patterns for increasing returns.

The primer for the next era of management will advocate the use of knowledge, sensitivity to market forces of all types, rapid adaptation, and the competence to emerge with capable strategies. Managers will see firms as systems in nature rather than as entities to control. Why so? The blunt-end rationalization or rigidity underlying optimization alone does not deal effectively with nonlinear dynamics and ill-defined scenarios of the future.

The business landscape provides a means to assess the complication and intricacies affecting a firm. It reveals the complexities the firm emits to effect market opportunity. In a world brought closer by a doubling of population in the last 50 years and the advent of interactive communication without regard to geopolitical boundaries, the landscape permits business leaders to manage change, voluminous information, and overlapping responsibility.

Business landscapes leverage knowledge so firms can comprehend the interactions and interdependencies determining their value. They discover pathways to new dimensions of value, then map them on the landscape for action. New templates guide action for greater precision and completeness. Business leaders tie negotiations to accurate forecasts derived from sophisticated databases.

Marketers and investors continue to target the increasingly attractive markets of South America and Europe, as well as the enormity of the virtual economy formed by the Overseas Ethnic Chinese Community. These are societies which greatly value relationships, prompting businesspeople to strengthen their interpersonal and cultural awareness of others.

Competence in the psychology of human understanding and acceptance is required for managing business relations successfully. In any society, appreciating how adults learn and shape their views of others can unlock mysteries for complex solutions. The greatest advancement for human relations in business may be grounding negotiation, joint planning, and dispute resolution in common sense and reality. The use of databases and economic models, heretofore scorned by "experts" for application in negotiation, may again debut to level the playing field. Fair play and economic responsibility will then supplant clever manipulation and irrational behavior.

In the twenty-first century, value leaders who create value for shareholders will be the masters of their business landscapes and partnerships. They will comprehend that a firm's relationships will co-evolve with its capital projects in value creation. Integrity will over-shadow image to command substance in business relationships. The appearance of success will no longer be sufficient. Managers will not oversimplify or ignore uncertainty, craziness, and diminution of value. Instead they will use the craziness, or the irrationality and dis-order, to their advantage. Trust and transparency among players will defeat the slick, the clever, and the self-deceit of denial. Businesses will carefully conceive and orchestrate relationships. Top performers in the twenty-first century will focus on the complexity which fosters wealth and will emerge with a life worth living for others and self.

The Human Touch—
Trust, Career,
and Chaos

In discussions about partnerships, trust is the most frequently mentioned characteristic of success. In our work, we talked about the fate of partnerships with executives across industries and cultures. The common denominator identified with success is trust between partners. Several executives made a point of including trust within the firm. Internal relations are also perceived as partnerships. More importantly, internal trust is linked to the performance of outside partnerships. Each owner in an alliance always questions whether commitments to the alliance will be honored and supported in a timely manner. The bottom line, in any case, is trust.

Consistently, executives describe external partnerships as taking more time and effort than owning and running their own operation. Merging acquisitions into a single enterprise is reported as less difficult than forming a partnership of separate entities. As much value as there may be in a strategic coventure—an alliance, a joint venture, a value chain collaboration, research consortia, whatever—the value is fragile. Here are what are cited as the opportunity costs for partnering:

a) There is less control over strategy and structure. Others have a say in how the new organization conducts business; even a controlling interest does not fully abate this concern.

b) Whatever the operation is, it will take longer to make things happen. Again, note the encumbrance of multiple parties.

The means used to manage and organize partnerships can minimize these constraints. Clear agreements on a shared business plan and how to execute the plan can offset concerns about control. Like in any business, the task then becomes stewardship of the business plan.

In practice, joint owners too often besiege partnerships with ad hoc reviews required by owners which grind business to a halt as they debate strategy in operational meetings. Competencies in conflict resolution and shared decision making are essential to investor relations in effective partnerships.

The employee involvement and trust-building strategy of a partnership needs review and discussion. Self-initiating employees can accelerate decision making or reduce the need for rigid control. Clearly, determining how to manage trust is important for comprehending the inner workings of partnerships.

Partnerships are subject to human frailty. When trust is missing, generating a profit requires more time and resources than when partners trust each other. People are more cautious, communication is likely to be impaired, gamesmanship finds fertile ground, and people cover up and deny mistakes. On the other hand, trust helps partnerships go smoothly and work past frailties.

Two other choices in human relations determine the fate of partnerships by setting the degrees of freedom needed for forming and operating successfully: career ambitions and the building blocks for trust. Let's examine the interaction of these to discover the impact of self-centered acts in contrast to teamwork.

The conceptual discussion is important for raising awareness of what goes on between people in partnering. The discussion identifies key factors influencing relationships. As you sit in partnership meetings or negotiations to form partnerships, you will better understand what is happening. At a minimum, you will be able to think through whether or not the relationship continues to make sense for your needs.

Early on, you will be able to describe patterns being set for the future in the relationship—by your partner or your firm. How is value grasped and acted on? What are the pertinent influences on value? How is risk managed? Who is trying, if anyone, to dominate? How is information shared? Who possesses the influence about what kinds of decisions? Where will effort come forth easily? When must effort be coaxed? What upsets? How is harmony restored? And so on.

The knowledge of emerging patterns will empower you to sponsor the outcome you value the most. It will be possible for you to set the direction or determine a response to the unanticipated. You not only will understand, but will have a means to articulate what is happening and describe likely outcomes.

This knowledge can make you persuasive. The knowledge will help you discern leverage points in areas such as the other party's career ambitions, views on governance, current preferences and understanding, and power to act. You will be able to describe probable scenarios in detail. Further to your advantage, the transparency you can bring to unfolding events will discourage gamesmanship and certainly make you less susceptible to manipulation.

At first the conceptual discussion may seem overly complicated. Sometimes we use new concepts or vocabulary, drawing on thoughts and terms others found useful in breaking down the complexity of human chaos. We then apply the understanding to human behavior in partnerships. We use what we see as the emerging common language for describing any system of nature or humankind. Coming from biology, economics, and physics, this process is known as complexity theory. Complexity theory is taken from the study of the chaos in nature and how order emerges from that chaos.

Our objective is to take you to a more sophisticated view; in the complexity, there is precision. Inherent to the precision in knowledge about other parties is economic advantage. You will create stronger partnerships based on genuinely-shared interest and benefit. Your improved understanding for the business play—whether it is technological, financial, or commercial—will permit you to see new opportunity. You will root out differences and tensions before they diminish value. You will sort through individual needs and appreciate how coalitions are formed. You will appreciate the impact of group expectations. You will grasp the essence of the opportunity and know what convinces others to join your pursuit of opportunity. Why? You will know the other parties, how they travail their business landscapes, and what motivates them to act or resist. You will know how to invite their ownership of an idea for results.

In the discussion of the psychology of career choices, we explore the meaning of human resonance, tone, and autonomy and discover how they influence the acceptance from stakeholders for any partnership. We explain acceptance by its impact on all stakeholders. We give special treatment to those closest to making the business relationship create value. For this reason, our discussion focuses on a partner's or the partner's employees' motivation to make the partnership succeed. Acceptance is understood for the role it plays in building shared responsibility for results—among partners and those working in the partnership. The goal is to have everyone involved feeling like an owner.

The building blocks for trust include transparency, learning, civility, and the way we envision commercial possibilities—a view we call the business landscape. The building blocks discussion reveals how to assess the quality of the relationship and build effective relations. At length, we explore the elements of a business landscape. We examine how elements interact and how to discern patterns affecting or effecting value. What we see as opportunity or threat is a function of our human perception. What we do about these possibilities is a function of our human choice. The bottom line for these topics is how people behave in partnering, regardless of the situation or its requirements. In your application to partnering, these insights will enhance your ability to understand, predict, and persuade. This is the human side of partnering in business.

CHAPTER 1

An Essay on Partnering—The 21st Century Strategy

SOMETHING OLD, SOMETHING NEW

The art of partnering is not new to humankind. It is as old as man and woman, brothers and sisters, tribe and trade. Originally, partnering in business brought to mind shared ownership among a few associates. The contemporary use of the term "partnering" describes a variety of business relations: joint ventures, alliances, research consortia, teamwork across a firm's units, and value chain relationships external to the firm such as supplier-customer action teams or customer intimacy efforts, attempts to know your customers' needs, goals, and motives. At the core, each is a human relationship focused on a shared business interest.

What Is New?

The complexity of partnering dramatically increased over the last 20 years. Extracting value from commercial efforts is growing more difficult. Fewer partnerships last. Many just drag along with performance below the expectations which caused their development. Growth requires complicated business relations to be even more complex as partners ask questions about continued participation, new participation, obtaining resources, and market access. Exits from partnerships are often turbulent.

For those able to unlock the mysteries of partnering, the reward is staggering. Often a relationship becomes a pipeline through which the original venture functions and many others follow. In a recent transgenic product launch, one product was the gateway to several more transgenics, the secure strategy of an existing product, and additional prospects in credit transactions and other technologies. The combined effect is multiples of the sales forecast for the initial transgenic.

In this way, yesterday's non sequitur in business development is tomorrow's value-added growth. What are important are the relationship, the potential for serving additional business, and the willingness of the partners to pursue the ventures together. Lucrative or not, complication is a given in partnering. The complexity surfaces within an enterprise as well as up and down value chains.

Human relationships are more involved in partnerships than in single-entity operations. Role overlap is higher. Loyalty may shift between owner and joint effort as the effort takes on its own destiny. The delegation of authority to enterprise units escalates accountability for managers at lower levels, many of whom are ill prepared for the new responsibility. Culture carries more weight in decision making. Tolerance and conflict resolution skills determine the fate of business relations as often as does the quality of the economic opportunity. The need for information and meaningful involvement is prominent in partnerships with employees. The human touch is multivariate and strongly imprinted on partnering.

The complexity of partnering goes beyond the human challenge. Technology is advancing in all realms—telecom, multimedia, Internet, computing, materials science, transgenics, biotechnology, and so on. Each has its own impact and frequently is dependent on other technology for optimal use. Consider advanced electronics as an example. The trend is not to invent a single new device but to develop platforms on which old and new technology combine to create yet another technology.

This interaction is demonstrated in the data broadcasting technology which uses the "backside" of a telecast band to convey large volumes of information to homes or business hubs. Software and hardware to "dial up" desired information will be connected to existing cable technology. Eventually, high-density TV bands will be deployed as well. With the data broadcasting technology, slow modems on personal computers (PCs) will no longer strangle the rapid transfer of high-resolution pictures and voluminous information. Advances in band management, cable systems, storage, and high-density TV make data broadcasting possible. Coupled with recent political decisions regarding the use of transmitting bands, the new technology unfolds atop the platform of the band's "backside." An array of partnerships among component designers and manufacturers will extract economic value from this overlap of technologies.

Many technologies impact how a company administers partnering. They expedite transactions, reduce operating costs, make monitoring and stewardship by multiple parties electronically simple, and provide separate and integrated financials with ease.

More importantly, technology innovation creates commercial opportunity for partnerships. The commercialization and global expansion of products and services based in technology are still developing. The revolution began in the post-World War II era and spurred onward by the Cold War and the Space Race, has yet to reach its peak. National laboratories with space and defense contractors continue to innovate—creating new commercial products from old weapon ideas or pursuing dual-use (that is, commercial and military application) technologies for the modern military. For example, research in "Star Wars" lasers has led to new waste management methods for hazardous chemical and nuclear dump sites.

In the pursuit of continuous innovation demanded by global markets, partnering enables technology advancement to be affordable. Industry players in research consortia distribute breakthrough costs among themselves. Nations place less emphasis on domestic monopoly to compete better internationally and thus use subsidy or tax relief to encourage sharing of participation in a technology. Frequently, no one player has the resources or knowledge for independent action. Then there is the question of corporate resolve to pursue research and development in the first place. As a member of a group, senior management may be willing to share in a risk they otherwise would avoid.

The globalization of markets presents constraints and opportunities which interact among themselves. New marketplaces may require local partners. A company may need infrastructure to service multiple regions and their uniquenesses. Outsourcing may make the most sense, or special relationships may emerge within the value chain to leverage one partner's infrastructure. Often partnerships are necessary to enter into a market or partnerships combine resources to complete a value chain. Financial engineering creates new and complicated business relationships in which equity and debt holders are difficult to distinguish by interests and practices. The complexity in commercial strategy is a trellis of interwoven opportunities and risks. Adaptation to the interdependencies within the trellis of global commerce is quickly becoming a core competency for management.

Regulation intersects to lace community and trade policy influence with business initiative. Legal, tax, and accounting structures for business relationships are more intricate and confounding to those charged to do the work. In the context for enterprises, liability is a specter shaping business decisions. Litigation and special interest lobbying influence business performance. Choice in sovereignty permits optimization solutions for levy, trade policy, and property rights—in particular, the growing area of intellectual property. There are simply more rules for business.

Human choice, technology, globalization of markets with complicated and overlapping regulations, all combine to display the complexity landscape for business. This spectrum for understanding and managing partnership relationships is a broad band. The band is subject to interference, chaotic turbulence, rapid growth, and opportunity accrued only with great precision. Managing these complexities is essential.

THE CHALLENGE IN MANAGING COMPLEXITY

The challenge in managing complexity is both to understand the complexity and to orchestrate a business response. The complexity demands extra planning, energy, and resources for success. At first blush, the demands seem overwhelming. A fear surfaces that focus and direction will be lost by overcomplicating business. In reality, addressing complexity produces a focus based in reality and sustains a business intent through the turbulence and randomness in the chaos of so much change—human relations, technology, global commerce, regulation.

Business analytics of interactions among influences to the business provide insight for a focus based in reality. Managers massage and interpret these analytics with the aid of templates. Templates facilitate focus on the shared ambition of the various parties. As the partnership evolves, the templates guide adaptation, learning, and practices. The outcome is timely action to accelerate the benefits of partnering.

This book responds to the challenge of complexity by sharing the authors' experiences with partnering across four continents. It addresses the common denominator of human behavior in partnerships and complexity. Trust, learning, and facilitation reveal the human touch in capturing value. The book is about how partnering works among people and how knowledge transforms chaos into economic order. Our final chapter defines scenarios for orchestration, making it all happen. Orchestration often includes learning, communication, and other business processing for getting the word out and preparing people to contribute their best. This shifts the focus to what is done to make partnering happen.

The business intent of the relationship, the parties involved, and the effort required define different types of partnering. Senior managers and most writers give the spotlight to large-scale partnerships or those involving decision makers among customers. As a result, most firms are very familiar with joint ventures and alliances. Chapter 6 offers a panorama of partnering solutions and promotes a common language among operators, deal makers, and executive sponsors. It further provides guidance on what some perceive as pedestrian relationships, those that are too often discounted because they occur at lower levels in organizations or are routine. These relationships, however, occur closest to the actual work and have the greatest influence on value performance day in and day out.

Throughout the book, case illustrations and war stories provide reflection on what experience teaches. Stories about partnering demonstrate how different circumstances influence outcomes. This knowledge will benefit decision makers in a constantly changing marketplace as they discover that adaptation to change is the most important determinant of continuous success and growth.

We do call to your attention the themes or characteristics which repeat, in particular, when associated with positive results. Some will call this benchmarking. For us it is simply the first step in determining what is possible. The best practice of the moment is best defined in combination with a better understanding of the market forces demanding adaptation.

Besides reflecting on past experiences, we guess at how you might need to adapt. We retell the wisdom of how winning patterns emerge for increasing returns in settings different from your own. In doing so, we suggest how to see and comprehend the vastness of your business landscape. With this practice, interpreting critical events and trends becomes easier.

We factor cross-cultural influences into inferences about what will work for you. We see culture as a business landscape dynamic warranting careful consideration. We base our suggestions on the assumption that fair play and sensitivity are inherent to the twenty-first century approach to business in any field.

This approach is based largely on our experience as practitioners and deal makers. Nonetheless, we express our ideas with concepts and models. When it comes to paradigms for managing complexity and partnering, we tell you our preferences. We admit to our failings and ask hard questions for the next time. We identify theorists, practitioners, and writers whose insight helped us make sense of real life. In all our insight and suggestions, our best tip is watch, learn, ponder, then improve and orchestrate and do it all again at the same time—continuously innovate. We show how this is done.

THE DRAMA IN PARTNERING

The excitement in partnering is the uniqueness of each situation. Experience counts, but it does not guarantee success. Vigilance to events triggers awareness, attention to detail prepares you for contingencies, and contemplation of "what if's" alerts you to possible stumbling blocks. In the detail lies a new precision and, therein, an economic advantage. The advantage will accrue only to those willing to learn and put forth the effort to analyze and apply what they learn.

As complicated as market economics, technology, and regulation are, they are easier to envision on the business landscape than human dynamics. Human dynamics needs attention in the management of a partnership. It influences how work gets done. Human creativity provides a rich resource for adaptation to the marketplace.

Where strong relationships already exist, this book may possibly present the first invitation to participate jointly in growth. The openness among friends in dialogue permits an opportunity to discern business intent. Collegial relations provide a willingness to be flexible in difficult times. The trust in the relationship makes interdependence easier to accept. A reflection on the advantages of strong relations sets a standard for any partnering.

Trust, transparency, and caring nurture partnering to create responsible, productive action. Different from everyday work, partnerships often inspire people to behave their best with others. Of course, with familiarity, the chaos of familylike treatment may erupt as parties are less reluctant to upset one another or air their dirty linen. Then partnerships can become tense. For these moments, business leaders need special conflict resolution skills. Fairness among partners is a hallmark while clever manipulation displays the mark of Cain.

Just examining strategic alliances alone among the many venues of strategic business relations, Fisher reports 20,000 alliances since 1988 in the U.S. with an annual growth rate of 25 percent.[1] Consider how the total number of mergers and other vehicles for partnering increase that number. We do know the 1997 world investment in mergers and acquisitions was $1.6 trillion.[2] Ernst and Stern report, "In the year 2000 . . . alliances are expected to account for better than 20 percent of the average firm's revenues."[3]

The odds are not good for partnerships among owners to succeed—joint ventures, alliances, research consortia, and mergers. Depending on the research or observer, the probability for failure is one-third or higher (see inset, "Studies on Failure," below). Why? From our experience, there are three compelling reasons: poor preparation, failure to manage conflict, and being overwhelmed by complexity. These factors often cause partnerships either to give up all together or to miss out on the full potential by narrowing attention to what is familiar or easy to manage.

In every partnership, there is potential for simple success or drama for distraction. In some cases, the theater of the partnership produces a creative tension generated from differences among the players. Properly leveraged, the tension yields innovation. Poorly managed, the partnering suffers. Minimally, the damage is a diluted focus. In the extreme, the partnership may break apart.

Economic failure is not the only reason partnerships end, however.

Studies on Failure

There is not a study or an exacting definition of partnering so that we know with precision what succeeds or fails. Difficulties in drawing sound conclusions increase when we realize that research is often based on no more than a few dozen cases. Generalizing to partnering as a whole with such limited research is not prudent. Based upon what we have seen and heard about firsthand, one-third of all partnering efforts fail. One-third realize poor to mediocre performance. One-third succeed. The studies that do exist indicate that patterns of partnering may create an order in which failure is likely. One study indicates that, in a partnership which has a large geographical overlap, the failure rate is 37 percent. The same study shows a partnership with uneven ownership split has a failure rate of 61 percent.[4]

Rosabeth Kanter, professor of business administration at the Harvard Business School, posits several reasons for failure within an alliance.[5] Most partners in an alliance fail to find "compatibility in legacy, philosophy, and desires" and only focus on the financial terms of the alliance. Another reason is the lack of appreciation of partners' differences at the same time they are looking at the synergy among themselves. There is also a lack of communication between upper management and the rest of the organization concerning the alliance. Lastly another cause is overinvolvement of the legal, financial, and strategy staffs and the underinvolvement of operational managers and their staffs.

The nexus of a partnership is the common goal. The nemesis to a partnership is the naturally occurring multiple expectations among parties. Prediction is seldom precise when preferences are diverse. This makes management of day-to-day business more complicated. The issue is whether there is an agreed-upon focus for operating the business. A focus sets a course, resolves conflict, and brings about reflection as the entity achieves results. From a lookback for testing the validity of the focus, the next value possibility may be seen.

Each day in partnerships can be a mystery. Partnering is an exciting, never ending story. New issues and challenges in the pursuit of value may enrich vitality or risk diminished performance.

The Marriage Metaphor

Many regard partnering as any pairing of talents and interests to a shared outcome, from marriage to business ventures to alliances between nations. The center of attention for this book is how executives manage complexity in business settings. The human relation learnings offered nonetheless have broad implications for a life worth living.

Corporate marriage can be as bewildering as matrimony. Matchmakers exist in both worlds with the same limited success. In a like manner to marriage, the chemistry apparent in the ceremony at the beginning of a business relation and the honeymoon to follow can be lost in a fog as the partnership enters gray areas and crosses time . . . unless the shared vision is clear and participants make efforts to renew enthusiasm. For couples and companies, it is hard work, fun, excitement, and acceptance of change which build enduring profits from the partnership and lifelong accomplishment.

We explore the human touch underscoring all relations in this book, giving equal status to business analytics, agreements used to develop partnering, and action plans to make the partnership work. The exploration of the human touch goes beyond the obvious to encompass creativity resulting from nonlinear relationships.

Choices important to partnering success often overlap. You need insight to understand what is happening and take effective action. For example, consider how complicated a partnership becomes where these issues overlap: how to sequence partnership proposals, the various forms of partnering, operating principles for partners, partner communication, how to measure and steward progress, the inner workings of each firm in the partnership, tax implications, questions of sovereignty, intellectual property rights, and trade agreements among nations.

HOW CAN YOU BE SURE IN A WORLD THAT IS CONSTANTLY CHANGING?

Much has been said and written about the way the world is changing. The technologies of telecommunications and transportation diminish the impact of distance. Interdependencies among markets and economies pass along seismic waves of turbulence or growth across political boundaries. As we have seen, the events in the Hong Kong stock exchange can be felt in New York in less than a day or, as evidenced by the 1991 Iraq-United Nations conflict, a war in the Middle East can set strong economies around the world into a tailspin.

Turbulence also exists at another level of life. Genetic algorithms plot our futures while human cellular transformations pose the peril of plague, or in contrast, decode into cures for chronic disease. As human density increases, we are locked into congested common areas, sit idle in gridlock traffic, and otherwise compete for life's scarce resources. We share thoughts, experiences, bacteria, and viruses because we are in close contact. Life was never simple. We know more about life than just decades earlier, but we know there is still much we do not know. Life adapts and emerges with new mystery. There are more of us to share in the experience of life; humankind numbers more than five billion.

How we fare in our relations with others—partners or not—will largely determine a life worth living. Relations will provide us with access to what we need and protect our interests. Those who understand and manage the intricacies within relationships and among networks of relationships will enjoy the economic advantages.

From the nano level of transgenics to macroeconomics, humankind is aware of more and needs to sort through gigantic information influxes. Partnering compounds the overload by combining multiple parties and creating exponential complication. For whatever is complex about one party is set in a matrix of possibilities among the partners. One's own expectations enmesh or collide with partners' requirements, views, practices, culture, and preferences.

Within partnerships, sluggish, collaborative decision making among partners puts success at risk. For this reason, we present business landscapes as a means for tracking your network of interfaces and their expectations. At a gross level, the detail is overwhelming. With templates and analytics, patterns emerge. From the patterns, understanding evolves. Common goals, operating philosophies, and a business plan can accelerate the decision making. These require forethought, dialogue, and joint planning. Perfect overlap among partners' goals is not a reality. Messy overlap with shared purpose and tolerance for difference is a probable solution. The solution can be fragile and warrants constant attention.

THE COMPLEXITY VIEW OF NATURE

Unlike pop business books, this view offers no half-dozen or so principles, takes much longer than one minute, and can outthink an empirical risk management graph.

Accepting the importance of messy overlap introduces a shift in paradigms. In contrast to linear, rationalistic models targeted for an exact "fit," a movement to use the nonlinear complexity view of events in business takes hold. The complexity view is natural and organic. By examining systems and their influences on one another in a natural way, you take into account their rate of adaptation, how new order emerges, and ways to shape patterns which eventually dominate behavior. These processes are not straightforward. They are

nonlinear and as likely to diverge as converge. What is most important in nature is a pattern which repeats, then becomes dominant,
forcing other aspects of life to adapt.

This natural view of life is more useful in observing change in markets than the old, linear approach. After all, markets consist of the
behaviors of organizations. Organizations set patterns they hope will
launch increasing returns. Organizations consist of the people who
choose the patterns, respond to patterns, and make them happen.
They make their choices at work and in partnering across the boundaries of the organization. People are beings of nature, not machines.
The natural, organic view should offer more insight as to how choices
get made in a chaotic, human world where more than five billion individuals set expectations for themselves, others, and the organizations
and institutions pertinent to their life. Simply put, in nature, order
emerges to benefit those who initiate patterns. The same is true of free
enterprise. The first to leverage knowledge of the marketplace is likely
to reap the greatest reward. Witness Federal Express and rapid delivery or Microsoft and MS-DOS or Windows operating systems.

Effective managers do not discard linear solutions but sustain
them to examine how they can optimize mechanical processes against
diminishing returns. The objective is efficiency and conservation of
resources through optimization. For example, Motorola continues to
emerge with new technologies but chose recently to align multiple
enterprises into two business units for more efficient operation.

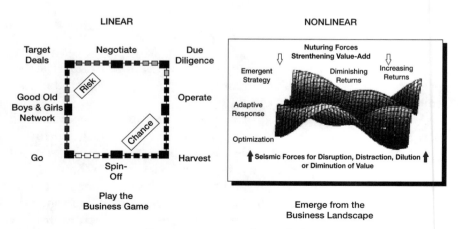

Figure 1-1. Paradigm shift.

The nonlinear understanding is brought to bear on knowledge-based business and the complex manner in which globalization and advancing technology shape all business. Multiple forces and interactions among them determine outcomes. Cause-effect, important in mechanical systems, becomes even more complex in this chain of events: there are causes, some more causes in interaction with the other causes, and lots of effects. When finished, the sequence is already happening again. However, these events do not occur in a chain; they are interactive and at times concurrent. Were this a murder mystery, the answers would be the lead pipe, the revolver, and the candlestick holder in a concert of action by Colonel Mustard, Mr. Green, and Miss Scarlet in the conservatory with passage through the library to emerge in the billiard room. Nonlinear challenges may be difficult to solve, but they are important clues to value. The objective with nonlinear solutions is to define patterns for increasing returns—growth into new facets for existing business or the emergence of new opportunities.

Over the last decade and a half, forces such as globalization, advancing technology, and financial engineering have precipitated adaptation. The experience taught the value of understanding how a small change in one part of the business world can impact other areas. Systemic, natural views of interactive influence have proven useful in formulating business strategy.

For example, the Legg-Mason fund deployed a rudimentary form of adaptive economics and landscaping business performance. The result is an impressive performance as a fund for more than nine years. In contrast to a field where stockbrokers rarely outperform chance guessing, Legg-Mason's $6 billion Value Trust mutual fund managed by Bill Miller "has beaten Standard and Poor's (S&P) 500 Index for seven straight years—(this) is a rare achievement in the investment world and proof that his brand of pragmatism pays off. In any given year, 85 percent of all managed funds trail S&P 500 earnings."[6]

Success in partnering is subject to the chaos of rapid change. Most noteworthy among the causes of change is the global marketplace. As a society, we are no longer in absolute control of the destiny for our own economy. Frequently we adapt to outside forces shaping our patterns of spending, buying, and investing.

Your preferences are on stage with many other players. At the end of the day, the speed of your genius to adapt quickly and emerge with your strategic intent establishes your quality of life. Surrendering and withdrawing from the world is not a choice.

Global competition will come to you regardless of your action. Today's choices are only in how to watch, learn, and respond. As you comprehend the market, you will understand how to leverage outcomes to your preferences. As your patterns set the new order and dominate, you can move from the ensemble cast to the leading player. Insight determines how to achieve increasing returns in the business of the twenty-first century. Business leaders need new core competencies to track market forces commanding adaptation, spot emerging opportunity, and set the dominant pattern for increasing returns.

Many feel partnering is the key to success though, as noted earlier, recent studies suggest that the probability of failure is high. To put it simply, the "cowboy" mentality of forming partnerships simply herds the players into the corral for negotiation but does not guarantee the expected value from operations. A mechanical use of templates and abrupt process may close a deal. The question is, can the deal deliver the beef?

The new order of management, from whom the leaders in the twenty-first century will emerge, will be masters of complexity in partnering at all levels. They will orchestrate multiple agendas at multiple points in the hierarchy in their cause to add value. They will use the same vocabulary in operations as they will in deal making and stewardship. All parties to success will then be able to comprehend what is happening, how value is leveraged, and what they must realize in their self-initiation to add value.

The leaders of the new order will guide adaptive business strategy and emerge with innovation. They will appreciate the importance of identifying interactions and interdependencies among causes and effects in their business. They will see the movement among elements of the business landscape—organizational, commercial, technological, regulatory—as volcanic activity erupting into new business formations or future markets.

Modern management offers many useful insights. Typically, however, business leaders and theorists prefer to avoid addressing complexity. There are two reasons for this. One is the desire to reduce the world to a half-dozen or so principles. Most often leaders derive these from observing what others have done. The words "have done" are the operative term. Would those who are deemed successful continue the practice once they changed business by this practice? Or would they continue to adapt and emerge with yet another new strategy? The only principles it makes sense to copy are core interpersonal communication skills and time management—personal work habits.

The tendency for oversimplification may extend to the management of product innovation. Contemporary business is faced with shorter and shorter product life cycles. New products are accelerating into markets ahead of consumers' ability to absorb them. While things may slow a bit to permit consumers the chance to catch up, the momentum for rapid change is set in the global marketplace. Solutions are not always replicated by competition as we saw in previous decades when long-lasting products were more critical than new ones. Instead, managers exceed today's success by setting patterns for the future through constant improvement or development of new market solutions.

You can easily memorize the half-dozen pointers found in most management books, but they do not possess the depth to explain a business landscape. They reinforce avoiding complexity by advocating simple explanation for complicated matters. We are not suggesting you abandon the wisdom from others' experience. We just suggest you not address complexity in business life with principles distilled from others' experience alone.

Not only is there an opportunity for the distillation process itself to dilute the insight, but the insight may not be valid in your case for two reasons. One is that the insight does not fit all the requirements you face. The other reason is that the insight, as already deployed in the market by others, may be forcing further adaptation beyond the strategy you might imitate. Repeating the solution of the other person may simply keep you from doing what is needed.

The second propensity among business leaders and theorists causing them to avoid complexity is an addiction to quantification. The first response to any business challenge is empirically to organize and predict. The risk is getting lost in the detail of the data and not interpreting it correctly. We have stopped clients from using assumptions from spreadsheets based on incomplete or incorrect formulas. In the quantitative world of today's business, it is too easy to believe the numbers and not think about what they mean. Harder to achieve is the reckoning of the numbers or the full appreciation of a business landscape. These take more thought and a broader view of events. The broad thinking across the business landscape results in a superior market position—a precise, reality-based view of what is next and how to emerge with increasing returns.

The other risk in a database-oriented view of value is to miss out on seeing what is possible. Innovation is seldom an extrapolation of the past into the future. More often, it evolves from a new and different way of seeing the world.

Thoughtful planning and preparation, articulating "partner fit," the selection of worthy partners, learning, dialogue, conflict resolution, and sensing the business landscape are now the determinants of value. The dominant pattern for success grows from the continuous process of adaptation and emergence. This new ecology of partnering is the charter for this book.

THE ORDER IN CHAOS IS COMPLEXITY— THE ORDER FOR THE 21ST CENTURY IS MANAGING COMPLEXITY

Managing complex choices in global business is a difficult subject to write about. How you describe the complexity of partnering and the way it impacts business decisions can mislead readers into believing that global business is a constant, something easily observed and ordered in a logical manner.

That is not reality. Partnering dynamics are alive and always changing. Their strength is measured by their flexibility and timeliness to respond to influences on a particular business. Their initiative is to gauge the level of achievement. Complexity in business is more crazy than rational.

Partnering is unpredictable. It is a blast. Partnerships are the fastest, biggest thrill ride in the amusement park called commerce. Like the thrill ride, partnering is not an experience for everyone or necessarily an experience everyone enjoys.

A few years ago an author on alliances showed us his mechanical, linear model for reviewing alliances and asked us for ours. We told him to split an old golf ball and look at the numerous, multicolored bands compacted on one another. This would come close to representing the myriad human interactions and business decisions in partnering at any level. There is no one mode to accomplish any business task. There are dozens and dozens of perspectives. A template exploring the completeness of a business landscape is more useful in practice than a model for drafting agreements or understanding economic valuation in a single context.

DNA and the human immune system are more useful metaphors than the models found in management books for business relationships. As complex as DNA and the immune system are, their workings can be understood for effective application. Their remaining mysteries are the frontiers for exploration. We not only need complex, organic views of organizations, but we would benefit from not being put off by either the complexity or its mysteries. They are merely future frontiers for mining value on the business landscape.

Our emphasis is on learning about adaptation and setting into play the patterns which lead to success. We offer hints not rigid paradigms. We do so because paradigms blind us to the forces of change. Models for us have value in teaching, not in prescribing. In partnering, the best coaching makes you aware of what fits together and how these factors influence one another. Visualizing the business landscape captures the interactions among business influences. Templates and their analytics help to digest and distill the information for focus. Understanding coupled with good judgment results in useful interpretation and knowledge for planning. A good plan drives action to results.

A CASUAL CONVERSATION ABOUT SHARING VALUE

Now it is appropriate to explain some things about the style in which the book is written. One is the manner of presentation. This is written as a conversation with a client. We are not writers; we are practitioners in deal making and consultants in strategic business relations. This is a practical guide for understanding human behavior in business relations, knowing how to watch the business landscape, preparing for partnering, closing deals, and making them work.

As consultants go, we are coaches and mentors for action more than lecturers, writers, or industry analysts. We are facilitators of the partnering process. We are keen on business analytics, but for us, they serve as a means to an end, value creation. We understand how to gather them and use them. Unlike analysts and economists who attend to business analytics full-time, we are more likely to accept the good work of others and apply our nonlinear view or abandon a forecast based on our analytics in favor of adapting to an emerging trend. For us, good analytics are worth more when forged into the reality of the business landscape.

With respect to how our expertise is offered, we want clients to know what we know. In a constantly changing world, codependency limits timely action. For this reason, we transfer skills for clients' self-initiation. Our intent for this book is to build awareness and skill sets for application on the job.

Our best medium is conversation because we are not trainers. We serve our clients in part by learning from them in dialogue about specifics, not just theory. What we suggest is a function of our understanding enmeshed with theirs, beginning where they are now—not where we want to be. In research, dialogue, and simulation, we are at our best, so we write like we are speaking to you as a client. For full benefit of what is written here, you should act like a client: do the thinking required to test the concepts against your business world and adapt them to your needs. The effort will produce insight beyond what is printed in the book.

Our conversations tend to be casual. If not politically correct at times, be assured we wish not to offend. We do want to make a point and we can be very direct and opinionated—not by the nature of our values and beliefs, but grounded in the reality of partnering. We are proud of our human touch. Our humanism is a part of our success. The human touch does not preclude value creation and return for investment. Indeed, humanism can ensure these results across time.

Another element of style is our presentation of ideas. The running text of the book carries the "meat" of our material. We take a cue from experts in displaying lots of information. We display complex information in different ways to allow you to digest the material as you see fit, knowing when we think there is a connection to be made by how it is presented and where. Look for case illustrations, war stories, and other insets. More like a magazine article, information is displayed to reinforce a point or help you visualize it.

REFERENCES

1. Lawrence M. Fisher, "How Strategic Alliances Work in Biotech," *Strategy & Business,* the newsletter of Booz Allen & Hamilton, 1Q96, p. 1.

2. "All Fall Down," *The Economist,* February 28, 1998, pp. 65–66.

3. David Ernst & Michael Stern, "Managing Alliances—Skills for the Modern Era," *The Alliance Analyst Home Page,* March 18, 1996, p. 1, www.allianceanalyst.com/protomail/newcap/mckinsey.htm.

4. Joel Bleeke & David Ernst, "The Way to Win in Cross-Border Alliances," *Harvard Business Review,* November–December 1991, pp. 127–135.

5. Rosabeth Moss Kanter, "Collaborative Advantage: The Art of Alliances," *Harvard Business Review,* July–August 1994, pp. 96–108.

6. Diane Banegas, *SFI Bulletin,* winter 1998, Volume 13, Number 1, p. 13.

CHAPTER 2

Trust in Business Relations

IT LOOKED EASY TO ASSEMBLE, UNTIL I GOT IT HOME

When we read about Exxon Chemicals' experiences in joint ventures, we were impressed. Reported in the spring 1997 issue of *The Lamp*, Exxon's shareholder magazine, Jim Lowe, Exxon Chemical Company vice-president for finance, information, and planning, identified among the many factors influencing success in joint ventures these four critical factors:

- Common objectives
- Comparable contributions
- Ability to recognize and benefit from cultural differences, whether company, national, or regional
- Strong support from partner management

What caught our attention was the succinct manner in which Lowe captured much of the opinion and research about working with partners. We contacted Lowe to learn more about his views. In our conversation, he spoke of an underlying theme to all determinants of success—the trust among partners. If you do not trust someone, he said, you probably should not do a joint project. Trust, to Lowe, includes notions like "straight shooter, fair, and no sharp tactics." This is the wisdom of an experienced player; many others are not so insightful.

Why see partnering as a complex issue if Lowe's view of partnering is clear and to the point? The reason is that concepts like trust, agreement between parties, fair play, the capacity to build on differences, and the willingness to support action are embedded in human behavior. Things are rarely straightforward between people—there is a lot going on between all of us, all of the time. Much as the toy to be assembled Christmas Eve looks more complex than the day it was purchased, you judge the complexity in partnering differently during operations than on the day you first considered getting together. Lowe's view is useful and valid. The distillation of human behaviors into partnering dynamics is complex.

The most complex human issue in partnering is trust. Its presence accelerates results. Its absence can easily destroy the partnership. We will examine how many of us see the concept of trust in terms of our lives, others in our life, and what happens when trust dissolves. The way we pursue career determines our potential to be trusted and trust others. We will suggest methods for building, sustaining, and when called for, restoring trust. In the case in which the partnership no longer makes sense for everyone, we review methods for determining how to leverage trust to achieve mutually beneficial exits from a relationship.

LOOK BACK ON YOUR LIFE EXPERIENCES— WHOM HAVE YOU TRUSTED? WHY? WHAT DID THAT TRUST MEAN TO YOU?

We have used the above questions in the subtitle for 20 years to kick off team building. The answers have been essentially the same over time and across diverse cultures and work settings. The single most frequently mentioned persons in life which people find worthy of trust are their parents, in particular, mothers. People feel distrust for parents strongly and typically are not quick to reveal the feelings. That is, they share parental distrust with great caution—probably because it admits to a deep, personal vulnerability. All in all, most parents are seen as very trustworthy. In these cases, this level of trust is held as a standard throughout life.

Our team-building dialogue elicits reports of close relatives who helped raise the individual, favorite teachers, and other life mentors as being trustworthy. As people reflect on adulthood, they mention loved ones, especially life partners. Again, if anyone feels betrayed, he voices it with obvious emotion.

Seldom do clients mention children as trustworthy. Instead, they refer to children more as those who place trust in the individual answering the question. Individuals are quick to explain why they are valued in their children's eyes. Someone usually mentions unconditional love. "I love my children regardless of what they may do. They know they can trust me. They are mine to love, provide for, and protect."

It is not rare for someone to list valued coworkers among the trustworthy. This is very true in partnership relationships where people spend a lot of time together or rely greatly on the other for success or survival, for example, law enforcement officers, business partners, and teams operating complex, dangerous equipment. When coworkers trust one another, they know a lot about each other's background and home life and are able to predict how the other will make choices affecting them.

Comfort in any relationship comes from the ability to predict. One aspect of trust and the ability to predict is not positive. "I know he/she/they will always cheat me," someone usually reports. This lament might be labeled negative trust, i.e., you can count on certain individuals or groups to hurt you. Oddly, in discussions of trust, people report this phenomenon and say there is still a level of comfort in knowing what others will do—even if it is bad.

What offers the most comfort is others keeping their promises. Here the dynamic of credibility enters into the picture as well. That is, will business allies make promises which they cannot or will not live up to? In some cases, a person may have good intentions, but no one really believes he has what it takes to keep his commitments. In other cases, people promise what cannot be fulfilled. We make our predictions as to whether we can trust them to deliver. This is a step beyond believing intention—it qualifies trust on the basis of whether a promise is credible to us. Later we discuss forgiveness as a means to restore trust, and the initial credibility of a promise as an important influence in the process.

So trust must have more to it than the ability to predict what others will do. In the team-building discussions, someone eventually describes trust as the willingness of another person to act on the individual's behalf. The intensity of the trust is measured by whether the trusted person will act in the other's behalf, even when it means sacrificing one's own interests to do so. If this is the case and the sacrifice is demonstrated, trust parallels the intensity of parental caring and is widely respected—by the beneficiary of the trust as well as others who hear of the situation.

What is amazing is the sense of fair play. By that we mean, with the notable exception of life and death endeavors, people do not feel you should sacrifice yourself or your family to serve their business purpose.

This is the odd place among relationships where trust at work is not managed the same as trust in family or intimate relationships. It can be expressed as, "I trust you to do right by me at work, but when it comes to self-sacrificing to the point you or your family might suffer, I understand if you must address your own needs first. You are off the hook with me."

This played out in the downsizing of the 1980s and early 1990s. It was not unusual to find greater guilt on the part of survivors than animosity among those let go. Middle-level decision makers anguished over their decisions to lay off friends and teammates; they were depressed at having let others down in their time of need. Those laid off, for the most part, understood decisions, even when decision makers could be seen as self-serving. That is not to say no one was disturbed or to infer this mature outlook was the first reaction. Once the shock subsided, however, the understanding for the situation prevailed.

To appreciate fully the dedication expected by some partners, examine life and death endeavors. From them, you can understand the value inherent in intense mutuality. Fortunately it does not always take a life or death dynamic to realize such expectations.

War Story

Signed, Sealed, and Delivered

The Navy Seals hold sacred the commitment that you do not leave a team member behind. This code is at the heart of an incredible competency in teamwork. A Seal once discussed with us a training exercise in a torturous jungle of South America among special forces units. Marine ReCon, Army Rangers, and Navy Seals competed alongside antiterrorists from allied countries around the world. The scenario was to escape from competing specialists with the full advantage of equipment and familiarity with the terrain. No one had ever eluded capture. An impossible escape route was pursued by the "prisoners."

Fatigue, illness, humiliating capture, and injury brought everyone down except two Seals. Their success was closely scrutinized in exercise debriefings.

Here is what was learned. First, the Seals had used an old Seal adage, "Take to the sea." They followed a stream, which led to a river, which led to the sea and freedom. But others had attempted the same strategy. Yes, the Seals were probably better trained at using water as cover. The difference among these survival experts, however, was not that great.

There had to be another explanation. The Seal reporting the experience said simply, "Teamwork." Though from different Seal teams, the Seals found one another and worked together. All others had worked independently. The Seals' reaction was, "Though we had not met before, he was a Seal and I could count on him." Wasn't this a theme in the film, *GI Jane*?

The lesson is that teamwork is based on trust and trust is based on teamwork. They are not the same. They are mutually adaptive. The rules of thumb are: the better the teamwork, the greater the trust; increase the trust and teamwork is easier.

It is also clear that colleagues and friends can achieve intense relationships of trust that most people reserve for family. Extraordinary circumstances, or special effort and energy, are required to achieve the highest level of trust. We do not have to cut our way through a South American jungle to become good team players; but we do need to make a concerted effort.

THE LANGUAGE OF TRUST

Another influence on trust, and a very subtle one, is linguistics. Many people do not have a sophisticated vocabulary for describing trust. At the onset of a conversation about trust, they stay at a superficial level or use simple labels to describe trust.

People banter about "trust" and "communication" when you ask why there is tension in a business relationship or dysfunction in an organization. In this context, these words are gross labels for wide ranges of behavior. Digging into their meaning reveals miscommunications, misunderstandings, feelings about belonging or resentment for exclusion, caring or being ignored, celebration or going unrecognized, and more. Having both good and bad experiences reported within the same situation is not unusual.

People truly know what trust is; it can be described very well if the right questions are asked. People tell you they literally can feel the experience of trust. On the other hand, most people do not have extensive training in trust. It is not taught well or not taught at all in schools, universities, or life in general. This is puzzling given that most people report trust as a key ingredient to business relationships of any nature. For that matter, the same is true of life relations in general. Given the importance of trust, should we not have more words to describe what is meant—words with strong common ground? Should we not find it easier to discuss and calibrate its intensity? Maybe schools and companies should give greater emphasis to learning about trust. Since we rarely do as we should, trust can be surreal, an image embedded in the craziness of changing expectations. Trust is something we want, define for ourselves, and rarely express in offering our requirements to others.

WHAT DOES CARING LOOK LIKE?

Another dimension of trust in relationships is caring. People demonstrate caring in their willingness to act on others' needs. You can trust some to take action in your best interest when given a choice. The question is, will they care enough to be proactive—that is, take action before forced into it, seizing the initiative to prevent problems or create opportunity? In the selfless act of caring, there is risk. You may end up harming the relationship with the trusting party. Caring sometimes requires actions or words which hurt feelings or cause resentment.

Preventing someone from taking an action on their own can obstruct their personal autonomy and cause resentment. Likewise, holding up a mirror to help another face reality can be overwhelming and hurtful to the person at the moment—no matter how useful the act of honesty may be in guiding the person to a more beneficial path.

Caring is the farthest step in trusting relationships, according to many. It is proof of wanting the best for another and making it happen—as opposed to taking action only when life collides with a specific need for trusting or to be trusted. It may take the other person time to see the act as selfless and useful to him. This is the stuff of paperback romance novels and soap operas.

On the up side, caring demonstrated to others produces a loyal following. People in firms report they want those who lead to care about them as individuals. When they believe that is the case, people are willing to dedicate incredible effort to support their leadership. Too many of today's corporate leaders do not understand this, and as a result undervalue caring as a leadership characteristic. Mislabeled for so long by organization theorists and consultants as paternalistic or pampering, caring for a time was shunned by experts as inappropriate career management. Then values and beliefs reemerged as important to business leadership.

TAKE ME TO YOUR LEADER— BUT ONLY IF THE LEADER CARES

What does the CEO value and believe in besides value-added performance and senior management's view of the market? Rarely is more known about a corporate executive than public policy and strategy. Clearly people want to know what makes leadership tick. Values, beliefs, life choices, and business decisions of the past are relevant in the minds of partners and employees. People are more likely to be less judgmental about a national political leader they can vote in or out than they are about the leader of their firm. Do not fool yourself; an evaluation is being made about the firm's leader. A "no" vote on a leader does not always mean an employee moves on to a new job or considers leaving. It is more likely to signal limited or no support for leadership's agenda.

Employees' trust in leadership accelerates progress and strengthens acceptance of strategy. Even strategies to restrain spending or calling for sacrifice receive broad support when coworkers trust leaders.

CRUTCH LEADERSHIP

Trust in leadership is important to most employees. By and large, these people are codependent on leadership for knowledge of what to do and how to manage risk. Without leadership to set a direction and focus, employees would perform activities, but the formation of their actions into a mosaic for creating value would be lost. Even in organizations in which direction and performance are clear, this can still be true. It can be true in organizations that encourage employees to possess a knowledge of the business that is sufficient for them to act on their own.

Codependence is a structural artifact of large or hierarchical organizations. The rest of the firm must rely on only a handful of people knowing enough to make good decisions. There are ways to improve direct involvement for some at lower levels, and they can act as representatives to the firm as a whole. Nonetheless, it is not yet practical for most firms to run their business without some element of codependence. Size precludes everyone from having the time or information for a timely market response and broader, direct involvement in strategy at the top. Hierarchy also strangles effective participation at the top. Responding to the boss' demands or a perception of what the boss wants can prevent sharing opinions or useful information for doing the job. Size and hierarchy leave most people in the firm with no chance for meaningful, direct involvement in strategy.

We recognize that codependency is the path of least resistance, the easy way out. Given the chance to prepare for the role of direct involvement and take it, a fair number of people prefer codependence. They like doing whatever they specialize in or do not want the burden of keeping the business headed in the right direction.

In any of these cases, the result is a heavy reliance on leadership's views. Everyone's future depends on how well the leaders call the shots. There is another potentially high cost of codependence. Dysfunction leads some to aim jealousy and resentment at leadership. Some people want to be led, but envy the reward and recognition granted leaders. This is just human nature for certain codependent people. A solution is to foster an atmosphere of teamwork with a division of labor and shared rewards. Everyone's effort should be transparent to others. Mutual respect should exist for the contributions made—large or small, direct or indirect.

It is better to have people think for themselves about how to do their job and have input into strategy formation, but look to leadership for direct decision making about strategy and action at the top. The trend to greater democracy in the workplace is healthy for encouraging self-initiation and teamwork. However, it is dysfunctional when the practice does not fit the work culture or is taken so far that management sacrifices response time and quality decisions for the sake of involving people.

War Story

Every Six Weeks We Make a Decision

We assisted a process chemical plant in the high-performance optimization of workflow and partnering strategies. The client invited us in after he had completed a self-help reengineering effort and the effort had faltered. The client, prior to our involvement, visited several organizations which achieved improved cost performance by phasing out layers of supervision and management. The client did the same, without the front-end investment of training and role transformation for the jobs above and below the roles eliminated in management.

In place of a management team was a mixture of four layers of the organization. The client required unanimous votes on all matters to make a decision, including operating matters other than immediate safety. Given their 24-hour shift schedule, the employees had overlap only for a couple of hours every six weeks.

It took the group nearly an hour to explain their situation to us. Another two hours went by with frustrations and complaints detailed in agony. We asked a few questions at the end. "Does your competition wait six weeks to make these decisions?" The answer was, "No!"

Then we asked, "Do you think you will be more competitive with such delays?" Again,

"No!"

"Look in the mirror; does this make sense to you if you owned this place?" "No way!"

We did not have to ask any more questions. The client returned management and supervisors to their old roles and the company implemented a learning-based transformation schedule over 18 months.

Involvement in the business is important for motivation, for gleaning insights from those closest to the work, and for management credibility through their being in touch. Involvement lacking meaning or purpose has little value. Involvement which creates bureaucratic decision making destroys value. Involvement from the top which meddles in the affairs of enterprise units, teams, and partnerships delays value creation.

TRUST AS WD-40™

One of the powers in trust is that it enables things to get done with less time and effort, and if trouble comes, trouble is spotted, understood, and either adapted to or eliminated as a distraction—in a timely manner. High trust, once established, sponsors self-initiation and makes agreement easier to reach. This is not mindless conformity. Instead, when everyone understands, acceptance results. Having experienced a trusting relationship in business, few are interested in anything else, provided there is choice.

Trust builds an atmosphere in which workers welcome or manage differences in views. By "welcome" we mean that difference causes no difference that results in a dispute. Opposite viewpoints are expected and accepted when they occur. Why? Either upset is not acceptable or experience has shown that differences are seeds of creativity. Looking at things differently may be a source of insight. Trust is managed in the sense that the appropriate communication or learning takes place to clear the air and get things on track again. Sometimes this is nothing more than admitting the distracting issue must go on hold until a better time, having made the commitment to address the issue.

In both public opinion polls and organization climate surveys, workers seldom rate leaders high for trust. If top management gets a good grade, those managers closest to where the work gets done will generally suffer in the ratings. There are compelling, interlocking reasons for this: hierarchy historically has not told the truth, all of the truth, or been timely in what it finally reveals. This is a lattice of deceit for most people.

Sometimes it is the top cloaking the truth; other times middle managers gag information and choke off upwardly flowing feedback. The other reason is that organizations are infrequently transparent. By "transparent" we mean that management permits people to validate the views and interpretations offered by leaders. It is rare for people in an organization to have timely access to meaningful information outside their function or department. Put into the context of partnerships, these dynamics are duplicated for each owner and similar barriers accrue between owners.

Transparency is a part of trust in leaders. People want to be able to predict their bosses and test the validity of the leaders' views with market reality. This is true for outside partnering—customers, employees, the community, shareholders, or business partners—the stakeholders for the firm. Stakeholders trust more when transparency exists. Then they can validate claims made by a partner's leader. Once validated, suggestions and action plans become more credible.

THE INVISIBLE MAN AS A PARTNER

If partners know what is happening and why, they can make their own decisions and have confidence their actions will support the other party's agenda. Transparency builds credibility and empowers people to adapt quickly or take necessary risk. Of course, it takes more than just knowing what is happening to build a sense of partnership. Partners must experience success and its benefits.

We are presently evolving to more performance-based and market-based reward for partnering relations. These range from incentives in the value chain to reduce cost and cycle time to employee participation in gains. We have not fully arrived, but the trend is strong. For employees, the strength of the trend comes from directly earning bonuses for their actions in the marketplace. This results in an experience akin to an owner taking profits and fosters entrepreneurial contribution.

For business partners, there is nothing like success to promote collaboration. What is pertinent to note is that greater access to independent, confirming information about a partner's choices enhances trust.

Transparency strengthens relationships. It improves the ability to predict. It offers confidence by permitting others to validate information. Transparency makes it difficult to pursue manipulation and exploitation. People can easily spot abuse, even in its formative stages. If necessary, transparency makes tracking the footprints of abuse much easier in investigations.

THE TRUST MYSTIQUE

Here is what we found about the workings of trust in business relationships:

The Essence of Trust

- Trust begins with the ability to predict what another will do. We want others to keep their promises.
- We draw on our childhood and adult life experiences to define trust.
- Trust strengthens as others act in our best interest.
- Most of us are fair; we do not expect self-sacrifice as proof of trustworthiness.
- Trust abounds when another acts at risk to self yet still proceeds in the direction of our own best interest.
- Caring proves others to be worthy of our greatest trust. They act on our behalf without waiting for circumstances to require a choice. Those displaying their caring may do so at a risk of losing our appreciation or affection. This is particularly true when a mirror must be held up to encourage reality in thinking.
- Transparency makes it easier to trust. Prediction is simpler. It is easier to validate that choices made are a matter of free will. Hidden agendas for personal gain are easily identified.
- The presence of trust in a relationship makes work more efficient. People rely on one another and genuine teamwork takes place with less distraction. There is great power in teamwork based on trust.

All in all, trust is the underpinning of our feelings about others. It influences the choices we make about how much we depend on others, what energy and resources we will put into a relationship, and where we will go in the future with others.

War Story

One Night on the Mongolian Steppe

In building strategic relations, it is easy to convince people to choose partners carefully. Preparation for negotiations and drafting agreements is hard work, but essential. What makes or breaks many deals and influences how they will operate is the human touch in the relationship. This is often overlooked because it is a soft issue with more folklore than good practice. To begin appreciation for the value added in the human touch, consider the story of an unlikely event in a distant land:

Intense human moments can build relationships which last a lifetime. A threat forces strangers and friends to face reality and pursue a critical path for survival. The crisis condenses human moments into a catalyst for transparency, civility, and trust.

An incident in Mongolia revealed the human dynamics of strategic relationships. A group composed of Asians, Europeans, and Americans representing 16 countries joined to tour Mongolia and Siberia. The common bond was an interest in cultural and commercial exchanges across the Pacific Rim. The travelers were professionals of every sort—lawyers, physicians, nurses, art historians, publishers, financial engineers, cross-cultural experts, political scientists, diplomats, performing artists, investors, photographers, artists, and others. Some were among the richest in the world or at least their country. A few were not new to adventure; most were accustomed to leisure travel.

Comic moments fostered a level of cohesion beyond everyday politeness at the onset of the group. Relations were beginning to build among this group of mostly strangers. On boarding a vintage Russian military helicopter, the travelers found not aircraft seating but carpenter's sawhorses covered with prayer rugs—stealthily placed between two large fuel tanks. The fate of passengers in a crash was immediately apparent to all.

Nervous laughter was muffled by the roar of engines as the well-worn craft departed the Mongolian capitol en route to Karakorum, the capitol of Ghengis Khan's empire on the mountainous steppes. Tension had begun to abate when a New York attorney mused that a crash would earn the headline: "Net Worth of Mongol 'Copter Victims Exceeds Mongolian National Treasury!" There were a few chuckles and then the passenger cabin was quiet except for the roars of the rotor blades and engines.

The travelers sighed with relief when the helicopter landed in the mountains. Those nearest the windows saw only a few Mongolian "ger" tents, the circular canvas homes of the nomads who make up nearly half the nation's population—no ruins, no lamasery, just three tents. The pilot appeared in the passenger cabin and persuaded all to stay on board as he ran off to the tents. Upon his return, the helicopter resumed its journey—now that directions had been secured. The realization the pilot landed in the middle of nowhere to get directions struck the group and laughter erupted.

Arrival at the appointed destination already included a spirit of survivorship. The flight had been quite smooth and without incident, save the "two peaks down and make a left" guidance from the tents' occupants. Even the passengers from the newer helicopters which did not land for directions seemed relieved. Imaginations had worked their charm, creating scenarios of what might have been with less luck. Acquaintances began to build the bonds typical of any experience of endurance and shared adventure.

The tour of the ancient city and beyond was breathtaking. The morning was rich with culture and natural beauty. In a place so remote and mystical in the view of the world, one could only feel privileged for the opportunity.

The morning was cool yet sunny and made the visit delightful. Lunch was a goat barbecue with typical local vegetable dishes. Quality was not important to the cook. Fortunately, the tour guides had Hershey bars to distribute. Then the announcement came. A forest fire near the capitol and high winds might delay the planned return. Casual conversation became more intimate as the possibility of not returning to the faraway hotel seemed real.

The Mongolian hosts made ponies available for the adventuresome while the majority basked in the sun. As five fellow travelers sat mounted on the ornate wooden saddles and stood in place for several minutes, a British traveler dryly remarked, "The marvelous things about these animals is they don't go."

Eventually they did. One young man entertained the group with his ability to ride with his body parallel to the ground and perpendicular to the side of the pony. His manner was so stoic that observers did not learn until later that his riding technique was without intent. A lady with considerable horse experience vanished at high speed down the plain of the steppe. The Mongolian hosts retrieved her unharmed, but her hair now resembled the pony's wild mane. Entertainment aside, the mood of the group was patient and accepting of the situation. More importantly, the tour guide had been forthright and transparent in communication. It might not have been the best news. Nonetheless, they knew where they stood.

By early evening, it was obvious that they could not fly out until the next morning. Again, the tour guide gave the message matter-of-factly and with a clear statement of what would come next. For some a gloom set in; for others a smile met the lure of an awaiting adventure. A few grumbled, but this was mostly anxiety talking out loud. The faultfinding did not extend to the rest of the group and almost always ceased when no audience offered much attention.

As darkness fell, the temperatures plunged. Enjoying a breathtaking sunset, the travelers became aware of their predicament and their most urgent need—warmth. Several ger tents were available at the landing site. A handful had stoves. Centered beneath an opening, the stoves provided heat throughout the ger. The layered Mongolian bedding provided comfort if you understood to get in the middle of what appeared to be a pancake stack of light mattresses.

Those who were attentive in the ger tours earlier in the day faired better that night. Those who used the western "princess and the pea" paradigm and slept atop the stack were very cold. The party of stranded travelers, at this point, was more a series of individuals and couples than a group.

The tour guide assigned tents. She placed married couples with other married couples and the few adult children with their parents. As best possible, she kept relatives with relatives and friends with friends. She assigned gender tents for those traveling alone.

The assignments seemed logical to several people, but the group dynamics typical of strangers set in. Requests to reshuffle tentmates besieged the tour guide. An odd mixture of concerns overtook common sense. These ranged from preferring to share space with those of the same culture or status to picking who would keep secret the sounds one's body emits in sleep. The swaps were made and some feelings were slighted. At most, it all served to be a minor annoyance, but the power of inclusion and exclusion had begun to work on nerves. For a time, the group was less than a group.

The count of tents with stoves did not match the need, so the guide dispersed a tent's worth of men to the floors of several tents. The relocation caused concern for one man with a bad back. Two new buddies quickly addressed his dilemma by moving a bed for him into his newly assigned ger. Such small acts of kindness were not rare. The press of the situation strengthened the spirit of cooperation. The mob began to evolve into a group.

A small band braved the difficult roads to a nearby village in an ancient bus to procure 50 toothbrushes and toothpaste. Why a store so very remote as this one would have such a stock of toothbrushes proved to be but one of several paradoxes for the night. No doubt the proprietor was pleased and forecast a banner year for dental hygiene products on the Mongolian steppes. Rumor abounded that the proprietor had a strategic business relation with the pilots or arsonists in the forests near the capitol.

The large ger used for the lunch that day became the gathering point and dining hall. Dinner was a meager recasting of the goat from lunch with noodles added for sustenance. The travelers greeted the meal with even less enthusiasm than they had at midday. The Mongolians' food supplies were limited. They did have cokes, wine, and whiskey available for purchase. No one would die of thirst and the body's radiator would have antifreeze of a sort.

Tent groups—better known as ger mates—sat around tables and enjoyed local singers and their own stories. It was then the important sharing began. The travelers pooled and shared candy bars, cookies, snacks spirited away from airport lounges, and mints. With a significant drop in temperature, Chanel-coordinated sweaters were of little use. More practical travelers willingly offered thermal underwear, bush jackets, and other apparel to create functional, though eclectic ensembles for the fashionable travelers.

A plenary discussion enlivened the evening. Observations about the worthiness of the pilots began with retelling the story of dropping down for directions. Learning there were no radios in two craft and no navigational gear in any did not enhance the credibility of the pilots and their crafts. Someone noted that no one uniform worn by the pilots matched another and the best pilot seemed to resemble a smuggler in a Harrison Ford film.

As the grumbling soared, it transformed into a brainstorming for alternatives to staying the night. Fuel limitations, darkness, much too old buses, the threat of bandits, and very difficult roads brought reality home. A night in the tent was forthcoming. Admitting this fact fused the group closer together. How to get on with the task of coping with the night got serious attention.

Throughout it all, civility was the choice. Acts of kindness, sharing, and caring extended beyond everyday pleasantries. When conflicts surfaced, the travelers demonstrated energy to restore harmony. Differences did not divide; they provided for interesting conversations, some memorable for a lifetime. The sharing of values and views was thoughtful and then insightful.

Some braved the cold and took the time to enjoy the deep blue sky and millions of sparkling stars in a Mongolian night. For a moment their busy lives were on hold. It was a time to reflect on self and humanity. The beauty of the moment could not be avoided. There were no distractions, no alternatives. The conversations were subdued, yet rich in insight. Beyond civility, caring and trust were maturing among group members. A peace settled on the camp despite so many shivering in their beds and hardly asleep.

Primarily a middle-aged or more mature crowd, most of the travelers made the trek to the common outhouse after midnight. Greetings were warm and friendly. The sight of another in such need spoke less to the difficulty of the situation and more to the awareness that all the travelers were human, no matter their worth, role in life, age, or gender. The bond was strengthened by this common human experience in a bizarre setting.

More comedy punctuated the evening. The Mongolian pilots, enjoying vodka, chose the early morning hours to serenade one ger. One of the evening's paradoxes would be the source of the vodka. The most critical complainer who voiced concern about the pilot's ability to fly ironically joined their choir and consumed his fair share. Other crew members occupied the ladies' restroom entrance and startled those seeking nocturnal relief.

For some accustomed to their bedrooms or at least hotel rooms, the tent poles were an unexpected obstacle in the darkness. Snoring was revered. It meant the ger mate was still alive and there was no reason for others in the tent to leave what warmth was gained to check on him. More importantly, snoring meant he was lucky enough to be asleep. Every camper compiled numerous war stories and told them at first light in a rush of multiple languages with a common laughter.

The morning after was uneventful, but the night had forged a community of survivors. There had been no real risk to life. There had been inconvenience and fun. A panic the night before or dissolving into subgroups to pursue riskier alternative plans could have produced very different results.

The return trip was uneventful. The community of ger survivors rejoined the other half of the tour. They wore the discomfort of no shower, shave, or make-up as a badge of courage. Oddly, the experience of the one-half did not divide the total group. The majority of those left behind took their turn at the helicopter ride, knowing the possible fate. Some may even have been eager for a like experience. When the two halves rejoined, it was clear the others had genuinely worried about those at risk. The half who did not experience the overnight adventure were an ever-so-patient audience for absurd stories, even those with meaning only to those who had been there. The event was the catalyst for the total tour group to merge and form friendships.

Several days later at the tour's ending celebration in Siberia, a prominent Asian business leader focused on the Karakorum event. In an eloquent address he retold the story to cement it in his audience's minds. He ended with an invitation to his home at any time for the entire group and dubbed them all his soulful friends. Others broadly shared and toasted his feelings. The warmth was in sharp contrast to the Siberian setting.

The lasting nature of the relationships began to show evidence soon after the group's return and separation back to their daily lives. The man with the bad back who needed a bed moved sponsored his new buddy with an introduction to modern taipans of Hong Kong. Months later, they exchanged e-mail and letters with photos with heartfelt invitations to be a guest in each other's home. One traveler invited another to a New York power breakfast to further a new friend's business exposure. Half-way around the world, a traveler kindly networked with a fellow traveler's good friend. They reported a marvelous welcome.

A simple travel experience showed the dynamics of a strategic relation. The tour guides were honest and helpful. They withheld nothing. They were transparent about conditions and their intent. For this, the group believed them and accepted their leadership.

The demeanor of the group was civil. They valued harmony, transformed differences to create acceptance, and resolved disputes quickly. They shared and cared. In the end, there was trust. The trust was sufficient for strangers to share a ger and sleep in peace; it was potent enough to build friendships. The strength of these relationships have great promise in friendship. The potential for cultural and commercial bridges in the future is quite high.

The travelers were a special group. They had a track record of extensive experience in successful strategic relations long before they came together. Even with this knowledge, they went through an ups-and-downs evolution to create their ger survivors community.

An external challenge certainly hastens strategic relations. Regardless of the time taken, strategic relations are built within the evolution of transparency, civility, and trust. Hard work will make the difference, and selecting partners carefully is fundamental to success. In the end, the human touch is what counts.

There is great fun and influence to be had in strategic business relations. Trust is the cornerstone. It is not necessary to risk your life in ancient Soviet helicopters flown by Mongolian cowboys to establish a basis for trust—but it won't hurt.

CHAPTER 3

Careers Can Add, Subtract, Multiply, and Divide Partnerships

WHY THINK ABOUT CAREERS IN PARTNERSHIPS?

When you are exploring a business relationship, understand the other person's career needs. This may explain what he wants. At the negotiating table, be aware of others' career ambitions. These can account for emotions and decisions you experience but feel have nothing to do with the economic merits of the deal. As you sit side by side working on bringing forth value from the relationship, comprehend the other's career circumstance—what decisions he can make, how he is motivated, when he will be rewarded, and where he may go next in his career. Answers to these questions explain hard work or craziness which distracts from value.

Throughout the relationship, appreciate the uniqueness of the other's career path. The sum total of this experience defines the context in which he decodes and understands your words. An engineer may calibrate and test assumptions. A lawyer may examine the unspoken for leverage in a commitment statement or perceive liability where you intend none. A medical doctor may expect declarations to go unchallenged by you, having given "the" opinion, and so on. For every career niche, there is a stereotype, and at times the stereotype may be valid.

Partnerships collect individuals or enterprises, and create a shared business interest. Enterprises are comprised of individuals and their careers. Careers are how work life needs and ambitions of individuals

47

match up with market opportunity. Partnerships are the sum of the careers of those working together.

To understand partnerships, you must grasp the meaning of the shared purpose in careers. The most basic partnership is between the firm and an employee. The greater the overlap between the individual's ambitions and the firm's goals, the more likely the employment relationship will continue, and continue with gusto. This extends to any partnering involvement the employment relationship includes: research consortia, alliances, joint ventures, value-chain teams, etc.

THE CAREER TRACK FOR AN ENTREPRENEUR

A similar dynamic is true for entrepreneurial and high net-worth individual owners. Their career is their enterprise. What happens to the enterprise directly determines their success in fulfilling needs and realizing ambitions. In a partnership, the alignment question is the same as in an employment relationship. What a partnership does to service career ambition determines enthusiasm for work and continuity in talent during the conduct of the business relationship.

This is best illustrated in consolidations by multinationals which acquire privately held firms for stock and cash or enter into a partnership. Many times the owner is kept on to run the business. In this case, the previously independent operator has some ownership but probably derives most of her income from an operating and maintenance agreement. The multinationals are dumbfounded when the operator behaves less like an entrepreneur and more like the typical employee. They forget an important truism: Bureaucracies can make a bureaucrat of anyone with enough time, control, and poorly aligned reward. If you pay a person to worry about presentations and appearances or focus on budgets and activities before results, you get what you pay for.

Partnerships cleverly meld different business advantages of the various partners. Global firms are seeking local firms to facilitate entry into markets. Large corporations partner with entrepreneurs to bring their spirit of commerce and efficiencies to operations. At the end of the day, the delivery of the advantage is dependent on the people involved. If those involved in making the work of the partnership happen are not aligned with the shared goals, the venture will falter— maybe fail.

Knowing how the players in a partnership view their career standing and what shapes those self-reflections is vital to the partnership. This is less a matter of creating unnecessary complexity, and more a case of reading the right map. Human ambition is a key determinant of success. When understood, knowledge of the human relationship predicts outcomes long before stewardship reports and financials.

SHEPARD'S VIEW OF THE FLOCK

The late Dr. Herb Shepard was a great mentor (see inset, "The First Corporate Elf"). He marveled at the complexity in human behavior yet offered understanding in proverbs and metaphors we all can appreciate. His insights about the relationship between trust and career remain valuable today.

The First Corporate Elf

Herb Shepard was the son of a Canadian accountant. In World Ward II, he helped soldiers, who returned frustrated and tormented from battle, to laugh and enjoy life again. He orchestrated theater and therapy to win back minds. The experience left him keen on studying more than his field of economics. He joined the innovative National Training Labs (NTL) to be tutored in force field analysis—a systemic view of life which saw multiple causes for human choice and human choice in a constant flux of change—under its leading author, Dr. Kurt Lewin. However, by the time Herb arrived, Lewin had taken a post elsewhere. Nonetheless, Herb found what he was looking for and eventually led NTL to success in application. He was among the many who shaped the '50s group dynamics laboratory learning effort in then Esso and Humble Oil, now Exxon, refineries and chemical complexes.

The massive effort collected the talented and some not-so-talented, self-consumed experts. This was a time before psychoanalysts became broadly understood or popular. In this case, very obedient professionals and managers from engineering, scientific, and business disciplines were placed in quasi-academic, quasi-therapeutic settings and told to share who they were. For the good of the company, they were encouraged to share their

innermost secrets. In the hands of some not-so-gifted, self-glori-
fying "experts," revelations and introspection appeared to go
too far in a few sessions for fragile souls. After suicides coincid-
ed with an event or two, the enthusiasm for the effort died in the
shadows of those deaths, as well as the entropy typical to team
building without renewal or structure. However, one initiative
endured because it made headway without placing people at risk
to their fragile psyches. This initiative was able to make significant progress by making the work place more productive. Herb
facilitated this effort which became the basis for the best models
in team building and career development. In the early '60s, Herb
emerged as a world-renowned consultant. He established one of
the first doctoral programs in organization development at Case
Western Reserve University and served as an icon and a found-
ing father in organized change. Most of all, he was a mentor to
change agents around the world. Jokingly, he spoke of his disci-
ples as elves and used the simile to teach the basic principles of
change work, for example, elves never work alone; elves are
invisible when they do their best work; and elves wear costumes
to fit the moment. His students took great pride in being called
elves. The man had a human touch and the ability to anticipate
like no other.

A few anecdotes: While instructing a beach house full of
change agents from across the globe, a sizable earthquake
struck. It was not of sufficient magnitude to endanger the group
given the special construction of the house to sway with the seismic activity. The danger would have been the panic. Given the
mixture of cultures, languages, and anxieties in the room, panic
was probable. Herb was speaking as the quake struck. He
paused with a passive and peaceful expression. As soon as the
first jolt and its associated noise subsided, Herb just picked up in
mid-sentence and continued. His demeanor defeated panic.
When asked why he had chosen this course of action, he replied,
"I did not know there was an alternative." Then he smirked.

To understand the grace of the man, you have to know he
lived the tenets he taught. Herb's house was known as Fort
Courage after the '60s TV western where misfits ran a cavalry
post and survived weekly dangers and mishaps with good

humor. Tired of always traveling, Herb built a conference center next to his main house to make visits there more convenient for clients. He also wanted a setting where people could be themselves. He did not hire professional builders. Instead, he gathered what some might call delinquent teenagers. Herb gave them a purpose, faith, and materials, then put them to work. The construction result was bizarre and comfortable. It resembled a frontier fortress. The human result was more impressive—young people found themselves and began productive lifestyles.

There were other oddities in the facility. A spiral staircase led to a merry-go-round pony and the indoor swimming pool next door. The bedrooms had swinging beds like on eighteenth-century schooners, made of wood boxes suspended on chains. And so on.

This conference center ran smoothly and corporate giants around the globe attended meetings there with fond memories of fun and insight. By the way, the delinquents would go on to run the center. One started his distinguished career as a chef at Fort Courage. They were known as "F Troop," the title crew of the sitcom.

Another story: Herb and his wife Tony, whom he loved dearly, were watching their son and daughter at play. As can happen between siblings, a fight broke out. Tony turned on the stereo and had daughter and son continue their struggle by dancing out their feelings toward one another. Soon the dance dissolved tension, restored harmony, and they began play again. Herb marveled at his wife's brilliance and brought the magic of the moment to audiences around the work. This was a man who invented and learned for every human moment.

One of his best contributions was to examine careers with the three things most of us strive to realize in our lives. The motivation to realize each is a force influencing career choices. The three are *resonance* among relationships, physical and psychological *tone,* and *autonomy* in how we use the choices available to us.

These are interactive forces which determine our sense of fulfillment as a person within our life's context. The three forces adapt to the context of life and reflect who we are in personality, competence, stamina, and emotion.

In work life, we look for access to opportunity from our firm to realize ourselves. If the context is empowering, we access the greatest potential for fulfillment. When our relationships are harmonious, we feel good and act by our own choice.

Shepard's contention was that we should all lead a life worth living, and work should not take away from our pursuit of a good life. "Empower" is the key verb for describing a firm's intent to enable its members—owners, managers, employees, contractors—so they may be their best. To empower is to explain business intent so well that everyone can self-initiate with the blessing of higher-ups.

For the most part, Shepard saw organizational life as working against our best efforts because people design organizations for controlling others rather than empowering them. While much has been said and written in company annual reports and management texts, the genuine application of empowerment is narrow. It is easier said than done. At least now the understanding of empowerment is growing.

An empowering environment strengthens the climate for trust. How we view our careers also strengthens our trust. Realizing resonance, tone, and autonomy to their fullest enhances our capability to trust and be trusted. Circular reasoning? Tautology? No, this is the adaptive view of the chaos in nature which recognizes the coevolution of two forces. Empowerment can enable trust at the same moment trust enables empowerment. So when we hear complaints about trust, we look to see what is happening—or not happening—with empowerment. The clues usually exist.

RESONANCE, AUTONOMY, AND TONE— THE RAT PACK

Long before the Santa Fe Institute was established to study complexity and talk of the adaptive and interactive nature of nature, Shepard envisioned the three life forces with the wisdom later found in the Santa Fe Institute's view of chaos and complexity. He saw the forces as constantly adapting to one another; that is, if relationships soured, they could affect health or tone. If a person became depressed, the mental depression could lead to diminished capacity, ultimately debilitating physical health. Likewise, disruptive relationships could make a person less effective at getting her point across to others because differences in opinion distract her or others. Furthermore, this conflict could dilute credibility since her words are not

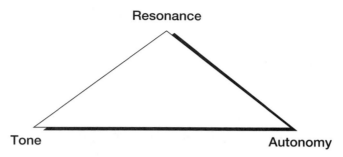

Figure 3-1. Life forces.

trusted. Regardless, this renders her less influential, thereby crippling her ability to accomplish her goals and thus, her personal autonomy shrinks. The adaptive, interactive nature of the force is continuous.

The interacting nature of life forces makes for complexity within ourselves and drives the complexity further as our wants and needs interlace with others'. Explore with us the meaning of each determinant of empowerment: *resonance, tone,* and *autonomy.* Reflect on your own life to grasp the impact one factor has on the others—influencing or being influenced through mutual adaptation.

Resonance in relationships begins with who we are. This means that how we see ourselves influences the manner in which we relate to others. The basic partnership then is with ourselves. If we are happy with ourselves, there is more in us to work successfully with others. If we are honest with ourselves, it is easier to be honest with others. More to the point, if we are mad at ourselves or disappointed, we begin each relationship with less capacity for responding to others.

The tension in our souls can be an inherent distraction to effective relations—the sort of tension we might not tolerate if it were the basis for a conflict between two people. For instance, if team members did not relate well because one did not like the other as a person, the resulting distraction to work would not be acceptable. As managers or coworkers, we would expect the team members to set aside the difference and return the focus to getting the job done.

At the core of all relationships is who we are to ourselves. As Shepard was fond of saying, we all have an elf in us. The elf is the fun, excitement, and enjoyment in our life. "Elf" is "self" without the "s."

Primarily, resonance is the quality of the bridges we build to others. If we are in harmony with others, life goes smoother. We communicate better. We tolerate more in relationships. This attitude allows more flexibility and broadens the opportunity for cooperation to take place. Greater understanding and caring enhance resonance. Resonance is essential to partnership relations, organizational transformations, and customer responsiveness.

Resonance is one dimension of trust. It indicates whether a relationship is going smoothly. In career, we should strive for the chance to build the harmony which makes resonance positive. Harmony makes it easier for us to trust others. There is less clutter to trip up the relationship. There is a better chance that the parties involved will set aside differences which pull people apart or that they will value differences for the creativity they may stimulate.

Harmony is rewarding. People who are harmonious are attractive to others. Harmony sustains relationships, permitting continuity. Lasting relationships reduce uncertainty and take fewer resources or less time to support growth. Harmony makes it easier to think and focus. The more positive resonance is, the higher the level for trust.

Tone is a composite of the physiological and the psychological being. It is a readiness to experience life—a reflection of energy. The greater our tone, the greater our vitality. It is difficult to feel threatened or fearful if tone is up. Tone is defeated with anxiety and frustration. Tone is undermined by illness and injury.

To some it is incongruent to say that illness saps tone when employees with serious, even life-threatening, illness can work with zeal—never revealing to others their suffering or pain. This is no paradox. This is the mix of the physiological and psychological forces that are tone. There are many cultures that believe people with faith can even cure themselves. Meeting the challenge to perform in illness is a part of staying alive, though it may require incredible energy. This is more than work taking the mind off pain and suffering. Purpose to life, as our work often provides, enhances vitality.

The composite of physiological and psychological itself is interactive. Illness can affect attitude and attitude can cause illness. There is further interaction with the context for life as well as resonance and autonomy. For example, a bright day can instill motivation. Good relations among a team can foster healing or restore self-esteem. Illness may reduce degrees of freedom, and outlook can build autonomy by identifying choices or motivating their use. Tone seems ever more confusing, but once you understand the possible explanations, you begin to sense each situation and search for the pattern. Then confusion yields to insight or comprehension.

Autonomy in this meaning is not gauged alone by the choices one has; how one uses his choices is also important. A person might not have all the money in the world but may still feel autonomous because he makes his choices well within the limits of resources available. Choice is the key to motivation. We explore this topic at length following a summary on the complex and adaptive interaction of trust and career.

COMPLEXITY, TRUST, AND CAREER IN A NUTSHELL

Trust is a complicated life process within each of us. Our basic learnings and our every perception shape our trust in others and how we may be trusted. Trust varies from circumstance to circumstance. It is not a Gordian knot to be sliced through to gain access to its mysteries as Alexander the Great did at the gates of Asia Minor. You must work through trust to appreciate it. There are aspects of trust in us we may never untie or cut through. Earning trust requires effort. It is only simple when achieved. Then trust functions as a wide highway on which many meaningful events may travel.

One life circumstance for trust relations is our time at work. Our view of career impacts our trust relations and is an important setting in which trust takes place, or does not. How we view our career helps us understand what trust will be. The career elements of resonance, tone, and autonomy are highly interdependent puzzle pieces. They shape our choices and move our energy for or against cooperation.

When we examine partnerships, we are exploring the intersection of careers. If we are complex as individuals, complexity is exponential in partnering. Numerous expectations run smoothly together or are at risk of colliding. It takes the wide highway which trust creates to avoid a wreck. In the following illustrations, review how trust reduces complexity when it is present and compounds confusion when it is absent.

Earlier discussion of tone may have left the impression that a sick person will not be as trusting or trustworthy because the illness can impact relationships adversely. Such a generalization is not intended. What can be said is this: Illness may make us cranky and irritable.

This temporary feeling may affect a relationship. Were the illness not transparent to another person, she could experience the crankiness and assume something is wrong in the relationship, more often than not, blaming herself. All this can be avoided with openness and patience. After all, we have all had cranky days, so empathy should be easy.

Relationships can themselves be impediments to other relationships. If there is a home life tension—an ill loved one creating extraordinary demands and exhausting a person beyond sensibility or an emotional upset like a spousal spat—this problem may create tension in work relations. When we encounter tension or others' performance failings, exploring the cause is a better tactic than responding with anger or antagonism. Trust is the pathway to avoiding unnecessary complications in an already tense situation. Start with the person, not the rationale assumed for the behavior. This advice is especially prudent in partnering.

Another illustration of career and trust is when a person feels he has control over his life at work. This sense of self-determination fosters satisfaction, personal fulfillment, and self-confidence. The good feelings then carry over to other relationships with friends, family, and even self. He greets people in home life with enthusiasm and joy. Good times have a way of finding a way.

FREE CHOICE MOTIVATES AND ACCEPTANCE MAKES THINGS HAPPEN

Autonomy impacts motivation in human behavior. If we act of our own free will, we tend to take responsibility and own the results. The feelings of possession and belonging inspire dedication or, at least, action.

In choice lies the question of the cause for action. If we are coerced, we take action but without responsibility or interest to continue once the pressure abates. A step up from coercion is compliance, doing something simply to satisfy a duty or an expectation of another. Repeated often enough, our actions shape a pattern and form a habit. There is a gray area in which compliance then becomes conformity. At that point, we feel a greater sense of responsibility and commitment.

Commitment is altogether a different thing from conformity. Commitment yields the motivation for powerful capabilities like self-initiation, endurance, and exceptional performance.

We can determine the motivation to act with enthusiasm by understanding acceptance. In 1991 Dr. Ken Organski of the Center for Conflict Resolution at the University of Michigan addressed the Society of International Business Fellows in Dallas. He reported on a model for examining effectiveness based on his research of war and civil unrest since the beginning of the nineteenth century. Today his method is used by the Central Intelligence Agency (CIA) to assess aggressors and their acceptance of reality such as in the 1991 Iraq conflict. Organski and his colleagues at the University of Michigan also applied the model to determining the political dimensions of the return of Hong Kong.

For Organski, *acceptance* is a function of *understanding, preferences, salience,* and *power.* He applied this concept to predicting decisions made by the state power utility commissions. We have applied it to decision making in organizations and partnerships. We found prediction precise when observers have insight into the decision makers. Pedestrian in contrast to the CIA work, this application is still potent.

Understanding is the ability to grasp what is going on. To comprehend evidence and see relationships among influences leads to acceptance. If you do not understand something, it is not easy to make a good decision or take the most effective action.

In human behavior, many people do not require much if any understanding before drawing a conclusion as to a **preference.** This is often the nature of prejudice. One way or the other, we will accept something more readily when it fits our view of the world, or our preference. If it does not, we need to be persuaded. At the heart of persuasion is building understanding for either a need to be different or a comparative advantage to be gained, warranting the effort to make the change.

The meaning something has for us is a measure of its **salience.** If the event is not mainstream to our life, we give it scant attention or care little about changing our preference. In this case, it is not a matter of acceptance but simply of passing tolerance. If something is likely to affect lives, we give it more attention. Should the impact be positive for us, we strengthen our acceptance for it.

The dimension of **power** in partnerships and organizations functions in two ways. There is the power to act and the power to stop action. When people feel in control of their lives, they are more likely to have acceptance. Powerlessness engenders resistance. Helping people to see they have power restores or embellishes autonomy. Feeling they are making a choice bolsters interest and support. All too often, managers act to control people rather than to empower people. From empowerment comes initiative and the quest for excellence. The same is true for partners. Partners feeling in control of their destiny will be more transparent, assume greater risk, and accept trust as a basis for a working relationship.

Motivation and its close cousin, acceptance, are complex human behaviors. It is clear to most of us what coercion is, but the question of moving from compliance to conformity to commitment is more challenging. The key is acceptance; acceptance is a function of understanding, preferences, salience, and power. When all four are positive, acceptance is probable. When one or more dimension is less than positive, complexity in eliciting action and initiative is probable. So is resistance.

How do we determine any of the dimensions of acceptance and thus discern motivation without feedback? We need a dialogue to calibrate understanding, to learn preferences and perceptions of impact, and to measure power—to support or obstruct. How do we successfully engage in dialogue if trust is not yet nurtured? Or how do we talk if relationships are not established? This sounds like the chicken or egg discussion. It is not.

The process of change in any relationship begins wherever the people to make the change are—not where others want them to be. You use these concepts to understand what must occur to make things work. The beginning is where there is the obvious opening and the greatest promise for success. Once you have a catalyst event, carefully encourage and assist in its progress. If trust exists on some level, begin there.

If acceptance runs high, move quickly on multiple fronts. If resistance exists, address it with communication and education, not argument. The goal is to introduce possibilities and make them credible in the eyes of those who must make change happen.

War Story

A Fish Called "SCAT"

One of the early supplier-customer action teams (SCATs) was initiated in a fishing boat. Two boyhood friends were operations supervisors in two plants which interfaced at a fence line as supplier and customer. Conversations began with which company was right or wrong. Their friendship kept the conversation from going past the faultfinding and blaming. They shared information higher-ups at that time would never share, not that there would be much detriment, if any. It was just not done. For the higher-ups it meant working at a relationship with no guarantee of a return—just the uncertain promise of a big bang which sounded like snake oil.

The two friends envisioned better ways of passing off the product by understanding one another's production cycles and costs. Sub rosa, they began to apply their fishing boat strategies. Two years passed before the SCAT was formed, based upon the progressive successes of the two friends. The lesson is: Begin where something exists, repeat the pattern, and adapt forward in the direction chosen.

If people are exhausted or mentally drained, renew their spirit with hope. This does not mean go-go speeches from senior management (too bad, they are usually unintentionally amusing). Communication will help, but the greater impact will be the proof of success. Launch experiments. Load them for success. This was Shepard's advice. Set a pattern for progress on which others may build. Advertise results to melt away resistance and doubt. Demonstrate learnings for replicating results and reaching beyond to new accomplishments. Create hope and challenge.

If people feel cornered and without choice, give them choice. Do not force beliefs. With subtlety, encourage by channeling energy and resources through meaningful information about the business, provide education with simulations, and orchestrate trial projects. Sometimes it takes a nudge and, as Shepard coached, you play god—but only a little.

Do not delegate for delegation's sake alone. Transfer skills and knowledge to ensure the delegation has meaning. Coach and mentor until a pattern of success emerges. Celebrate progress and recognize group and individual accomplishment.

Be aware of your urge to force things. Understand the limits of traditional command and control. The very best will catch on and go along in command and control. They are the elite who aspire to your leadership role. As for the rest, just enough may trail along to give the appearance of change. Their sluggishness along with the resistance or ignorance of the rest drag out the process of change.

We often hear about how to manage resistance. We try not to let it get out of hand. Resistance spins out of control when too much force is used. Then a backlash reaction results.

Even the elite may secretly support the backlash to "fit in" and win acceptance from the "troops." We find in these cases that resistance is less the issue than ignorance. Communication and education were missing. Not enough was done in the beginning to build momentum. A slap on the face with reality and a nudge in the direction of safety are proper when a fire is burning in the room. Such coercion is seldom inviting to bright, decent self-starters when times are good.

We are always amused by expert's statements about transforming organization cultures. Their predictions range from five to ten years. They base these predictions on the aforementioned phenomena and the size of the firm. This limited view of people perpetuates the myth that transformation takes a long time. We know from experience that the proper front-end communication, education, and design combined with careful orchestration of the pace of change and celebration of progress can accelerate results. Important and enduring change can take only a matter of months when you understand the complexity and address a framework to guide the new performance.

We were one of the very first to address accelerated organization design and reengineering (see inset, "Accelerated Change," on p. 61). We were initially criticized until our projects brought in results months ahead of similar ventures. Acceleration is necessary for change to occur. Planning and the right investments make it happen. This takes understanding complexity and hard work to orchestrate. (See inset, "Accelerated Change.")

While each of the above cases resulted in a transformation in business, we must make two observations. One is that these were units of a global firm and not the entire firm. These efforts would be experiments and experiences which fostered change elsewhere in the system. Part of the task of orchestrating transformation is breaking it into pieces which can be managed for rapid change, and staging change so it spreads.

Accelerated Change

In three different operating units for Monsanto, we assisted the redesign of work systems and organization. First was the Rhone-Poulenc-Monsanto JV acetaminophen unit producing the base chemical for popular pain relievers like Tylenol. This effort was completed in about nine months. Similar efforts elsewhere within Monsanto and other companies were taking two to three years. Using case illustrations from successful start-ups and redesigns, a cross-section group called a design team completed optimization. They also formulated an orchestration plan and detailed team building and training. Done on a part-time basis in place of the norm of full-time teams for a year or more, the design adapted ideas and created their own solutions. In time, improvements in quality, cooperative efforts with regulators, and productivity enhancements resulted. These results were competitive or exceeded accomplishments of the longer-term endeavors.[7]

Events moved even more rapidly at the Fayetteville plant. The facility was periodically faced with the possibility of being closed. The efficiencies resulting from the high performance design reestablished credibility as a producing unit and additional capital investment was made to the site. This design team completed work in less than six months and began to show impressive results within a year. Again, results were more than competitive. Site energy and waste partnering with other organizations and providers would set a trend for other locations to follow.[8]

Not long after Fayetteville, the model was replicated in the expansion start-up and owner turnover for a business unit in Australia. Marketing interfaces were included. This location exceeded earlier applications, taking just a few months to complete the design work and within a year demonstrating bottom-line results. Impressive to this application is the record-making cooperation among union and management. In a few days, they were able to close on the innovative agreement in what normally would have taken many months. The introduction of performance-based rewards was accepted with the investment in education for broader responsibility. This site achieved competitive accomplishments in performance as a result of the design team's plan.[9]

What was probably most notable in these efforts was the clever use of others' ideas with the freedom to explore unique solutions. Others' applications as offered in template and case illustrations were not posited as the answers, but helped, along with the briefs, to accelerate learning for the design teams. In place of starting with a blank sheet of paper, the templates and case illustrations moved solutions forward quickly. There was little frustration in contrast to the blank sheet approach on previous projects. Surprisingly, the ownership for results was actually better.

The other observation is that transformation occurs in fulgurations. These lightning-like jolts move the unit to a new level of accomplishment. The growth however does not end. Growth is an inherent, continuous dynamic of the new order.

Further to this point, longer-term transformation tends to not reach as far and as fast because of two extremes of the same process. On the one hand, there is so much happening, taking so much energy that longer-term efforts overwhelm. It is difficult to change if you are just keeping your head above water.

To the other extreme, longer-term efforts take so long, the change is not seen as real. Avoidance is easier because programs come slowly. They can be avoided or undermined with ease. Real change comes from a material and economic reason for change, surrounding a firm with the change by altering in simultaneity the core work systems and providing the learnings and resources to succeed.

In a very different setting, we have helped entire large systems with sales over a billion dollars to change in a year and one half. It need not take a decade, if the investments are made and senior management truly supports. The punch line to all the cases in the war story is career life can be changed. The change need not take forever. The better you can adapt in career to change, the higher your probability for success—now and in the future. At the heart of all partnerships are the careers of the people who must make it happen.

A career has no legs without the capacity to contribute, and the willingness to adapt.

Change is an organic process. You watch it carefully and nurture what works. You jump in to address misunderstandings and get things back on track. You steward closely in the beginning to prevent things from falling through the cracks. In it all, you lead with hope, a vision of what is possible. As a career dynamic, change is to be managed. You explore with it. You position with change. With change, you emerge into new contexts for value.

The point is to understand these concepts and survey your business landscape. Begin where it makes sense and make things happen. A positive pattern repeats success and promotes further adaptation for improvement. Fail to set a pattern and the process will be random. With or without intent, patterns evolve in nature. Business is no different, just another aspect of nature. Patterns can be either good or bad.

That is why it is important to make choices and set a business intent. Following the direction you set, the patterns supporting progress will then emerge.

Each cascade can be stronger and better than the one before—if you will, a pattern to patterns. Careers have patterns. They too can be by choice or occur with random order.

Luck is being in the right place at the right time. In moments of modesty, people will talk about being lucky, not good. Our observation is that very few people get ahead by managing their career as though it were a lottery pick. Most are very purposeful if they do not get distracted. We advise you to choose the right patterns and hope they are aided by good fortune.

THE KALEIDOSCOPE OF LIFE

The complexity in human behavior is staggering. A potent core influence in adult behavior is career—its habits, choices, and external influences. One's expectations set patterns which are overlaid on others, much like a kaleidoscope. A turn of the cylinder and those expectations change, adapting to the new patterns as well as some of the old.

Trust, career, and acceptance are interrelated dimensions of human choice. They build complicated motivations for intricate human behavior. Consider, for example, acceptance. It is enhanced by understanding. Understanding is easier to achieve in a trusting environment. Trust is a foundation for career but also is derived from career perceptions. That is, people will be more trusting if they perceive less direct risk to their personal career.

However, there is more to acceptance than understanding. Preference, power, and salience play a role as well. One may understand an issue, but the understanding could butt up against preferences, power, and impact to self. Observation must be incredibly keen to predict accurately when there is low trust and little dialogue.

Thinking through the expectations for just one person can be overwhelming. Life is not simple. What we do is complicated with interactions with others possessing their own expectations. In everyday life, we try to predict not just how one person will react but how groups interact, whole organizations behave, and communities and nations resonate together. At this collision of expectations, we find complexity.

COMPLEXITY CAN BE A PANE

Susan Ballati of the Santa Fe Institute likes to share how Nobel laureate Dr. Murray Gell-Mann explains complexity by envisioning a normal distribution curve for the molecules in glass. At one extreme is a pane of glass—uniform and rigid. At the other extreme is the gaseous state—random, chaotic, and turbulent. In the middle is complexity—the fluid state which can easily cool to a pane or heat to gas. This is the area of flexibility.

We offer a related metaphor for the flexibility in the middle. This is the territory for art and judgment. Just as a glassblower can bend, shape, and craft molten glass, we can choose to adapt or emerge with our craft in complexity. Glassblowers can create beautiful figurines, shape useful bowls and glasses, or produce precision glass containers for science. In life in general, complexity can be artistic and abstract or very precise with an architecture for focus and action.

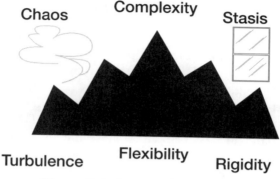

Figure 3-2. Stages of complexity.

THE RISE AND FALL OF EMPIRICISM

Since the turn of the last century, business has been enamored with quantification, from Taylor's scientific management to today's risk management models for derivatives. These approaches work best in closed systems in which optimization against diminishing returns is important. People and the ways they organize are, in contrast, organic. They are constantly interacting and adapting. Human interaction impacts every business transaction. In aggregate, these transactions are economies. Economies function as open systems. In globalization, economies are interactive and adaptive among themselves. For example, the downturn in Asia at the end of 1997 was felt to at least some extent in the West and elsewhere. Some say the effect will ultimately be more than "some" extent.

The lesson is that empiricism, basing everything upon experience, will not work in periods of anomaly. Events in open systems are more subject to forces prompting adaptation, the effect of anomaly. The process is like the weather. During the weather ambiguity created by El Niño, someone bemoaned the inaccuracies of weather predictions of a day or more in advance. El Niño is an anomaly. The use of forecasting models based on previous years will not help. The interactive forces of weather are situation specific, in particular during El Niño. Doppler radar can portray the weather landscape with accuracy as the weather is experienced. Assessing the landscape and integrating judgment about the forces at play can be beneficial within a narrow time frame of an hour or so. By the way, here's a tip: Do not align your reward system to the ability to forecast.

The enormity in the collision of human interaction does not wholly defeat the value that quantification provides. It does present the need to use judgment. In complexity, the most valuable tools are observation, understanding, and insight. The art is identifying the patterns emerging as trends and opportunities. An aid to judgment is knowing empiricism is limited when adaptation takes place. That is, inferences drawn from data on past behavior may blind us to the adaptation which occurred or is occurring. In such cases, we do not act on what is, or could be, accruing.

The great value of the human touch is that it makes things easier: communication, sharing of information and resources, tolerance for conflict resolution, and creativity. You can identify value when you study the landscape on which business takes place and identify pathways to follow which optimize progress across the landscape. Or the study may reveal a mosaic among pathways and events. We use optimizing models as tactical tools; strategic decision making belongs best to those who see the patterns. As potent as math models can be, they do not supplant the power in trust and the advantage of good judgment.

Before getting too caught up in the superiority of perceiving increasing return, remember that judgment is fleeting and may be more a matter of style. Value can come for a time—namely, the Andy Warhol 15 minutes of fame—from style. Style is a form of judgment, but its endurance is the capacity to ride the wave of the next trend. Judgment about what is right then changes. There is no one answer. We just resolve that judgment in value is not always consistent, rational, or, itself, enduring. The message is: Once you find the pattern, keep searching for the next one. Your career vitality will depend on the search.

Trust too can be violated and lost. The value in trust is the capacity to endure, repair what gets broken in a relationship, and control important emotions influencing our tone and resonance. Trust is a continuous process and not a state of being. A state of being can be violated or lost. A process continues as long as the person cares to do so. A process requires constant attention and energy. In career, we must work hard at trust and build relationships capable of meeting future challenges.

War Story

Tattoo or Not to Tattoo

The linear assessment of health hazards regarding tattoos is: Do not get one. As a young colleague is quick to point out, the decision is, however, based on more than one straight-line conclusion. In the mosaic of personal fulfillment, style, the daring of the moment, the fraternity of those bearing tattoos, trust in a professional, and the social possibilities made available from conversations about tattoos, they all say, "Yes!" Be mindful; there is judgment and, then again, there is judgment. It is less than a perfect world. Each of us has his or her own complex of prejudices and preferences.

The moral to our story is that judgment is an adaptive process. It is influenced by attitude, belief, and the events and people surrounding you. There is tremendous career opportunity in spotting the emerging patterns and knowing how to extract value. Remember, however, that not all patterns are enduring. Further, controversy between conservative and liberal views tends to be uni-dimensional. Dialogue and appreciate differences. In a partnership, it is rare to find everyone in agreement about tattoos. To some, a tattoo is a mark of great beauty. To others, it mars a great beauty.

All in all, the math in careers is very complicated. You must learn whatever you can and hope it all adds up to something, ideally something better than when you began. A calculator will be useful since formulas for success change and complication increases. In a partnership, everyone arrives with a career stored in memory and a lot of expectations about career exponentials.

The strategic business relationship is a merger of careers. The merger can be like a great Scottish battle for freedom in which much value is destroyed trying to defeat the powers that be or it can be a ballet in which body and soul master a harmony with grace, style, and exceptional career performance. It is your calculation to make.

REFERENCES

7. Fred Kokemor, Ken Petit, Tim Poche, Ken Stanton, Eugene Vallery, and Gary Ralls, "A Return to Quality Leadership: The APAP Story," *The Ecology of Work Conference Readings,* June 5–7, 1991, Ed., Janice Newman, Cathy Slack, Tom Chase, p. 2-32–2-40.

8. Fayetteville Design Team, "The Monsanto Fayetteville HPO Model," *The Ecology of Work Conference Readings,* June 16–18, 1992, Ed., Janice Newman and Tom Chase, p. 5-1–5-7.

9. Design Team, "Monsanto Plant Design Report," Monsanto Australia Limited, 1994.

CHAPTER 4

The Building Blocks for Trust

STACKING YOUR BLOCKS TO SPELL "TRUST"

Trust expedites and strengthens strategic business relationships. Understanding the elements for trust provides a blueprint of what it takes to create a capable partnership. We present the element of trust as four building blocks: *transparency, learning, civility,* and *the capability to envision the business landscape.* With an understanding of trust, the task then is making trust happen in the relationship.

Our metaphor of building blocks is accurate because each element does build on the other. The format is misleading in that it implies this comes first, then this, then that, and finally this. That is not the case.

The building blocks are adaptive and interactive with one another. Since trust in a new relationship does not begin in a vacuum, we cannot sequence where to begin and go next. Previous relationships and perceptions shape and determine how trust will unfold.

Trust is not found at the end of a linear progression. Trust dynamics are much like the processes in adaptive cognition—how we think and deal with the world. We used to think cognition worked like this: sense, think, then act. We are now certain sensing, thinking, and action are always happening and these dynamics are always adapting to each other, i.e., thinking is shaped by actions, actions are shaped by what we sense, and so on. This is a continuous, interactive process. Trust too is a continuous, interactive process. What is accomplished in business relations can be lost or strengthened as the dynamics within trust—transparency, learning, civility, and the capability to envision—affect the status of the relationship.

In most circumstances, all of the building blocks will be needed to effect lasting trust. Their interaction mutually reinforces and evidences that the context for work is based in trust.

TRANSPARENCY—THE 21ST CENTURY OPENING

Transparency between two people means they know information about each other's backgrounds, preferences, knowledge, and opinions. Acceptance for a position on an issue is a function of credibility. If we have credible experience—i.e., we were there, we studied the subject, we heard from a credible source—we are usually judged to be trustworthy and our views found to be useful. The sharing of who we are determines credibility. The process of sharing builds transparency.

Interestingly, we have worked in many businesses and partnerships where people have known one another for decades, yet people cannot tell you much about their colleagues. When we do our work, we first become familiar with the people in our client company. This strengthens rapport which is the key to obtaining the whole story. Without a close relationship, valid information is difficult to obtain. We learn more about the potential of people, why they may make a choice a certain way, and what is convincing to them. All these things take very little to discover and greatly aid communication and relationship building.

Some of our colleagues and clients claim the opportunity to establish rapport among coworkers has improved with the advent of flat and lean organizations. Our experience is different. Yes, some places are a bit better in terms of knowing one another, but by and large, things have changed little. Though bureaucracy declined with flat and lean structures, roles are more encumbered. As a result, people are less interested in sharing information about themselves becauase of limited time and a mindset that such activity is soft, offering no return in the eyes of their bosses.

Additional evidence that sharing backgrounds and interests is less valued can be found in how young people who are new to an organization react. Asked what is important, they tell you getting the job done. Is knowing about your fellow worker in the venture important? Yes, to a little extent. They do not want to be seen as nosy or taking too much time away from work by being friendly. How does this view help if we are ever more dependent on one another and our partners? History repeats itself when we do not take the time to learn from our mistakes. We are in danger of warming the leftovers of traditional organizations we claim to have dismantled. Weren't traditional organizations shunned in part because they were too distant and cold?

Transparency is more than knowing one another well. Interpersonal transparency comes naturally to some people. For most, openness takes many years, and as we said earlier, it may not occur at all. Team-building exercises accelerate this process. Skilled facilitators can be useful to ensure the process is complete and timed at the appropriate point in the evolution of the relationship.

On a group or organizational basis, transparency requires more. It is knowing the business intent of the partnership—whether within a firm or between parties in a joint venture. Transparency includes governance: Is the information made available in a timely manner to stakeholders? Does this information permit stakeholders to have confidence in management and the direction taken? When people can align intent with what is happening, the credibility of leadership is excellent.

Michael Hudson, president of Rolls-Royce's U.S. subsidiary, Allison Engine, sees governance as critical to success in several ways. One way is that senior management sets the "principles of agreement" from which a company determines the final terms and conditions. Lawyers and staff develop details and set metrics and performance targets. Senior management uses these to assess progress. Senior management uses progress reviews to sponsor adaptation to changing markets and lend support to the venture. Ensuring support within the parent firm for the venture includes career support for venture managers. They must have sufficient prestige to get staff functions and operations attuned to the mainstream business.

Further, Hudson sees another role in governance for senior management in the firm as aligning venture managers to support their sponsoring organization's quest for value. By career counseling and proactive coaching, venture managers remain focused on value created for the parent firm.

Hudson notes that the role of governance carries special responsibilities. One responsibility is asking the hard questions about the quality of prospective partners, the business worthiness of a plan, the "fit" of the venture to core competencies, and the potential for disruption by market, economic, or political forces. Sometimes senior managers must ask these hard questions of their prospective partners who may be less mature in business acumen. "After the initial glow fades in long-term relations, there must still be a business purpose."

Sharing information is not yet routine in strategic business relations. Businesses overuse the excuse of proprietary information. They barter information for influence and favors. The outcomes of leaving people out of the loop are eroded trust and rumor filling the void. Risk is not managed well under these circumstances. It is easier in business to share information in a thoughtful, purposeful way. What does this look like?

Whatever You Say

Hodja was a thirteenth-century wiseman in Turkey. Over the years, his mythology has been emboldened and his reputation for wisdom valued from Siberia to Northern Africa. Here is a story of Hodja and the Sultan, Tamerlane:

One day Tamerlane invited Hodja to his palace for dinner. The royal chef prepared, among other dishes, a cabbage recipe for the occasion. After the dinner, Tamerlane asked, "How did you like the cabbage?"

"It was very delicious," complimented Hodja.

"I thought it tasted awful," said Tamerlane.

"You're right," added Hodja. "It was very bland."

"But you just said it tasted delicious," Tamerlane noted.

"Yes, but I'm the servant of His Majesty, not of the cabbage," he replied.

In every organization, people know who runs things and what is cabbage.

First, have partners—internal and external—sign confidentiality agreements. Align reward and recognition so everyone genuinely experiences the business relationship as an owner would. (If they are already owners, stress the shared destiny aspect of coventuring. Show people they truly share risk with you.) Give equal emphasis to the responsibility and psychology of being included in something greater than self. The involvement will be meaningful to many. Educate people on the importance of belonging to the relationship and the disaster of misused information. Be clear on what is improper and demonstrate the opportunity associated with being in the know. Be diligent in the enforcement of agreements. This includes prosecuting those who may be involved in the purchase of confidential information, e.g., competitors, activists, disgruntled former employees. Be public in managing abuses. Let people know you take confidentiality of information seriously.

When it comes to sharing business information, do so in a general manner so it is understood only on a broad basis. Some people have been successful in telling the big story without revealing any information that places the firm at risk. How much more gets shared? Whatever the person needs to be self-initiating.

Keep the information vital. Share results periodically. As is often done, show variances between what was planned and actual results. Invite feedback. Ideas and opinions may be very useful. An important value-add from transparency is the dialogue it creates about what to do next.

When problems exist, make them known. Do not hide the unpleasant. Shift norms so that problems are treated as challenges, not as faultfinding and blaming. There will be some of that—such is human nature. Make certain the conversation gets to learning and action planning to solve problems.

Above all, do not attempt to disguise a management foul-up. Put it out with a confession, not a rationalization. People may not be stupid, but they can oblige you by appearing dumb if you try to fool them or treat them as though they were dumb. It is sometimes easier for people to accept being treated as dumb than to risk confrontation or take the time to change a manager. Of course, this is not new to humans (See "Hodja" inset, page 72).

Is this pie in the sky? No, we have clients who have shared intricate, intimate information at all levels. They experience less abuse than those which are very restrictive. A command- and control-dominated venture will often foster abuse and make such abuse hard to discover. One of the advantages of transparency is that fraud and abuse are discovered faster. Why? More information about what is actually happening is known by more people who care about what is happening—or not happening.

War Story

Transparency: The Fraud Buster

A major fraud in expense funds had been perpetrated in a large, foreign joint venture. Finance and accounting systems were stretched by explosive growth in the multibillion dollar megaproject. Despite audit, the abuse went undetected until accounting clerks and secretaries brought the abuse of professionals and managers to upper management's attention. Much more was lost because those knowledgeable had to build courage to come forth, not so much out of fear of retaliation but because they feared carrying the message to bosses. Only when an effort at transparency and teamwork was encouraged did the theft get reported.

An amusing note on the subject of transparency: More than once, we have encountered firms and ventures which were very restrictive, only to discover that their most precious information could easily be distilled by analyzing public information from customers and regulators.

Halal offers insight to leveraging transparency in corporate communities. Corporate communities are united internal and external partners on the value chain. Such communities leverage social responsibility, business ethics, and cooperation to achieve competitive advantage. They pool information to optimize work systems to a "common repository" for research and operations improvement.[1] They appreciate the value inherent in sharing information with partners. The value stems from a fundamental human aspiration—to belong.

Making the Team

Think back to when you were a kid and playing a neighborhood game. How did it feel to be chosen last—or did you ever have the experience? Every one of us has experienced the joy of being included and the disappointment—maybe even resentment and anger—of being left out. It is a powerful dynamic which changes how we see ourselves, the shared destiny, and work itself.

If we are honest with ourselves and are not sociopathic, the feeling of inclusion is very important to us. Look at society to judge the notion. What are street gangs about? Why do people spend a fortune on club memberships—even after the IRS no longer grants write-offs for memberships? Why do people proudly display alumni rings or sport school ties? The need has been in our genes a long time—family, tribe, community, nation. We identify who we are to a great extent by the groups we belong to.

When we belong to an enterprise, we expect to know what is happening. We want to know what will determine our fate. Sharing information is important, proving we belong to the firm. This recognition fosters motivation and caring for shared success.

Exclusion is the fast track to not caring, maybe reprisal. At a meeting of executives for a presidential commission on cyber terrorism, discussion focused on the threat of vengeful employees. Numerous cases of physical and cyber abuse by the disgruntled are already on record—many more are not reported to avoid consumer concern or embarrassment. The incident rate is increasing. While we do not want you paranoid, this is a reality. Employee resistance to strategy and practice is even more likely. The subtle and constant erosion of work effort by employees stems from being left out.

From baby boomers to Generation Y, today's work force is increasingly more self-oriented at work. The downturns of the 1980s and 1990s eroded loyalty to the firm as cutbacks and business closures left thousands without jobs. Many begin their careers tuned out and socially isolated. Work needs to catch their interest and draw them in. A caring community at work strengthens employee commitment.

This is not a return to paternalism. Our recommendation is for a fair partnership in the employment agreement. It is also smart economics, as entrepreneur Ira Rennert discovered. The architect of turnarounds for prestigious institutions such as the Harvard Alumni Fund invites meaningful employee involvement. The involvement results in shared reward based on market performance. The invitation to be included is a powerful motivation. The value added is that huge debt gets paid back faster when employees participate in the gain and value can be extracted sooner from capital deployed.

LEARNING—THE PASSPORT TO THE 21ST CENTURY

Learning influences all partnerships. Learning fosters understanding so people see the value of collaborating. The learning process promotes the knowledge necessary to build a partnership and keep it operating. Learning sponsors continuous improvement and innovation to develop and grow the partnership. In the partnerships internal to the firm, learning is proof of a bond between employer and employee. Employees value the learning investment as a demonstration of the firm's interest in them.

Our discussion of learning has two parts. First we examine the process of learning. An understanding of learning will help you appreciate its merits and vulnerabilities as well as the importance of properly supporting learning with multiple methods and repeated exposure. These investments are necessary to move an entire group of people to a new level of knowledge and its application. Then we move to a discussion of what learning is needed.

Part One: Learning about Learning

Every experience promotes learning. Learning is a positive environment in which formal and informal relations grow. We learn when we read, attend a class or seminar, watch a TV show, see a film, view a demonstration, or participate in a conversation. Learning influences how we see the world and relate to others—in firms, partnerships, markets, and communities. The invitation to shared responsibility promotes enthusiasm and the exchange of ideas.

Trust is a function of learning. If you want to change someone's level of acceptance for an issue or project, help them understand your position. Inform them. Teach them. Coach them. Preparing and orchestrating learning is fundamental to partnering. At the heart of persuading your partners is helping them to learn. Compelling a partner to comply with your demand based on the interpretation of contract language or coercion engenders resistance. Building understanding, on the other hand, is a catalyst to shared responsibility in addition to compliance with your request.

What is learned is sometimes simple, but the process is complex. It begins with the fragile nature of human communication, which is at risk of psychological distraction. The noise created by our differences in background or ambitions can mask a message or dilute its meaning. The complexity is in our heads. At once we are sensing, thinking, and reacting. The dynamic of learning is a part of our thought process, which is continuous and interacting. Were this not complicated enough, we learn in different ways. What works for one person may not work for another. This variance, by the way, can cause conflict.

For some reason, we want others to value how we learned something. We want them to experience the same growth we realized. How many organizations have suffered through replicates of the CEO's best seminar experience (see the war story, "The Boss's Wife, the Guru, and Us" below). The seed for the CEO's fad of the day is a genuine interest to reach people with an important message.

The difference in learning styles can interfere with the learning. Some can achieve learning from reading a book; others need lectures and coaching; still others need hands-on experience; and so on. And sometimes we are not yet ready for that particular learning.

The CEO has his or her own knowledge base and access to information—comparatively more generous than that to which most others in the firm have access. The CEO may have been ready to learn, but the rest of the organization is lost, confused, or simply not prepared to listen in the same way as the CEO. Worse yet, there may be another fad in six months to add to the confusion.

Things are further complicated because the pace and amount of learning which can be absorbed are not the same for everyone. These differences leave people at different levels of understanding and motivation to act. CEOs need to remember to start where their employees are, not where they were before they experienced the learning.

War Story

The Boss's Wife, the Guru, and Us

At a major oil company in the 1970s, the spouse of a senior manager became enamored of the meditation techniques of an eastern guru. The character was right out of The Arabian Nights—pointed beard, pastel Nehru jacket, turban, and curled-toe slippers. A Hollywood costumer could not have done better. If his full program were adopted by the company, it would absorb much of the various educational budgets.

From each of the major affiliate companies, one or two representatives were called to participate in a sample seminar. They were either trainers or internal consultants. The powers that be told this group at the beginning of the session that they could be apostles for the guru if things worked out. The real reason the group was chosen was that the powers that be surmised they were not putting much at risk with these particular people. Nonetheless, the group would satisfy upper management's demand that the presenter be given a serious audience.

The instructions to participants were shrouded in mystery: be in the headquarters building at nine; casual dress would be permitted—a rare privilege in those days. The participants encircled a conference table and followed the guru's lead. By midmorning the group was humming and chanting away. During one of the eyes-closed mantra chants, one colleague fell asleep and o-o-h-m-m-m became a loud snore. The fellow-up discussion polled the group's reaction, which would double as an official statement for their affiliates.

No one knew whose spouse was behind this so some participants perceived the risk to be high. The representative of one of the most conservative affiliates gave a diplomatic critique. He personally found such methods innovative and envisioned meditation to be useful for those facing a great deal of stress. He felt, however, that the need in his affiliate was very narrow. There was not much stress and people knew already how to handle what stress existed. (This was at the time of a major energy crisis and wholesale lunacy abounded in any oil company.)

The representative continued with a possible concession. If another affiliate were to sponsor a session, he might find an interested party or two to attend. He concluded with the statement that he personally had no immediate need for stress therapy. His open briefcase on the floor behind his seat revealed three rolls of antacids and a bottle of laxative.

Outside the room the colleagues all agreed they had wasted a day in their very busy lives—not because they found no value in meditation. Some already had reputable teachings available in their training and development programs. They did not appreciate not being told ahead of time why they were issued an official summons to be in the room; more irritating was having to suffer the con artist's mediocre presentation of a meditation technique. The crowning blow was the spouse referral. Accustomed to the executive fad of the month phenomenon, the representatives feared a whole new avenue of distraction from work—spousal imposition.

Most wished the guru, the spouse, and the powerful executive an experience which will remain untold out of politeness. The participants wanted to even things up. No one invited the mystical presenter to his organization. No one really put much effort in raising a red flag on the waste of shareholder value.

It would be good if we could say executive fads are in the distant past. To do so would create a really funny story.

Hey, Mister! Got Any Change?—Crisis, Context, Mentoring

A leading family psychiatrist once explained that there are two important psychological processes in reshaping our way of seeing things: crisis and mentoring.

Crisis—The Power in Walking the Plank

A crisis presents us with a need to survive. When we confront the reality and accept it, we are usually willing to restructure how we see things. For example, a heart attack may bring about an improved health regimen. In a similar vein, the 1980s and 1990s brought a rude awakening to most of American business. Declining profits, the success of competitors—here and abroad—and takeovers made American business reckon with the need to change. American business fundamentally changed the rules by which it structures work and pursues opportunity. Crisis prompts a response.

The start-up of a new organization or a product launch can foment a "crisis" mentality by creating a sense of urgency. So much is different for many people sharing the experience, their behavior is characteristic of a crisis situation. There is a rush to get organized, get going, or produce results. Though these situations are growth-oriented, a fear of failure prevails. We can expect this in most partnering situations since partnering tends to pursue growth or enmeshes many people and their expectations.

The crisis must be intense and enduring to bring about change beyond the individual level. Groups are prone to be mutually reinforcing—even when they engage in denial. Partnerships among enterprises tend to do a better job at reinforcing themselves than individual firms do. One party or the other will demand performance and challenge the discrepancy between reality and denial. This may not always be true, but the chances are better with a partnership. Individual firms are more susceptible to denial since there is not an offsetting influence of a partner. Bureaucratic interference with the upward flow of feedback in single-owner firms compounds the problem.

The psychiatrist says that mentoring reaches back to our growing-up experience in which trust existed with a parent or teacher, some adult who cared and sponsored learning. We trusted these mentors dearly, and they taught us our fundamentals. They made us challenge our overly simplistic, childish cause-effect views and accept reality. When we trust someone and find them credible in a subject, they can be convincing to us. They facilitate our understanding and help us reach to new paradigms.

We add to his view our experience in accelerated transformation of firms. In our work we have seen the importance of crisis and mentoring but often find fundamental change without crisis. As noted above, start-ups and product launches create crisis-like responses. These and other situations significantly alter the context of work. Mentoring couples with a comprehensive change in context. Structures and systems of work change; management introduces new vocabulary and policies to describe how work will be done. It becomes difficult for anyone in the system to avoid change.

The psychiatrist argues that so much change could be a crisis. He feels this is not playing a game of semantics. The speed at which change occurs and as the amount of change can be overwhelming just as a sudden or prolonged downturn in business or a disaster can be. When overwhelmed, we are more open to change.

Context—The Power in Moving Furniture

Systematic change in the business environment can result in fundamental changes in beliefs if the context is broad-based, sustained, salient to the person's life, and reinforced. Forming a partnership can be such an event—at least for those who immerse their careers in the partnership.

Partnerships change the context of work with important influences. Now expectations for performance come from more than one party. It is not easy to get past more than one set of eyes. Multiple owners are multiple resources. Money, time, insight, and energy for making things happen come from more than one source. Mutual expectations are powerful determinants of business choices. In partnerships, it is not uncommon to find people on their best behavior. They do not want to show the other side what they can really be like.

With multiple owners, planning and budgeting are not more rigid, but people complete these and other processes with more fervor because one side or the other might complain. Communication can be more involved with multiple parties, but parties may exert more effort to make it happen. This includes documenting the business activity, tracking performance, and ensuring that instructions and feedback are shared. The work to identify immediate improvement and formulat capital deployment decisions usually gets more attention in a partnership. Innovation and relationships with third parties are similarly given more attention to detail and follow-through. When all parties develop and agree on a business plan, its implementation can bypass the delays attributed to multiple owners. Such delays are less the function of multiple owners per se, and more likely attributable to distrust, poor planning, and concerns for direction in the absence of a business plan. Done correctly, multiple owner problems dissolve and the advantages endure.

All in all, the context for work in a partnership promotes, within the mutual expectations, an atmosphere for doing things with the appropriate communication. "Appropriate" is a key word. Partnerships closely scrutinize staffing and resist bureaucratic layering inside the venture. They recognize multiple owners already burden a joint effort with different approaches to administration. No one wants to add to the problem. The proclivity of large owners to add layers in the parent organization to service the alliance, however, is a different matter. This is their choice and not a burden to the alliance unless there is an attempt to charge back the cost for the overheads to the alliance.

Building trust goes smoother when there are multiple efforts to influence with crisis and mentoring and by changing the context. Mentoring introduces reasons to collaborate, provides coaching for effective teamwork, and sponsors relationships where none existed before. Changing the context of work to value transparency in governance, risk taking and initiative builds opportunities for trust to develop. A company can exploit a crisis to jolt people into valuing an atmosphere of trust.

The shift in paradigm emerging for Western business from command and control to empowerment illustrates this phenomenon. The command and control way was just not getting things done. The willingness to try something new was less motivated by the belief that empowerment works and more by frustration with the status quo. Regardless, empowerment in action emerged into a pattern for success. Progress sold people on the value of empowerment.

In contrast are the corporate "lip-syncing" image managers. The right words are in the annual report, used in every senior executive speech and in all employee communication. They are voiced but not expressed in behaviors. The result then is, at best, confusion. Disappointment abounds. Doubt emerges. Unfortunately this is still the dominate pattern in organization life.

Changing the context does not always help. We all know it is possible to partner with someone who does not deserve our trust. We can make money but probably not as much were the person trustworthy. Situations in which there is low trust require more time and energy with less comfort. Attempting to avoid a bad experience with untrustworthy partners may lead unnecessarily to onerous legal agreements.

The downside to the use of protective agreements is that a pattern of distrust develops. Terms and conditions restrict conduct within the relationship. This makes trusting relations as laborious as those based on distrust. The context defined in any agreement should fit the relationship and not be a boilerplate to defend against all adversity.

War Story

How Many Lawyers Does It Take to Screw in an Agreement?

We conducted interviews across the U.S. for a client with a different partner in each region. A consistent complaint was the rigidity of the legal agreement. The partnership was too good to pass on although each regional partner had reservations about the agreement before signing. The complaints were quite similar. Little was left to trust. In all four cases, the other side searched for clever ways to use the rigid agreement to get an edge. A great deal became just a good deal, and gamesmanship triumphed too frequently. To get even, one party did not bring the full advantage of a value-added service to the partnership. Another manipulated performance within a service agreement.

Internal Change—Partners Within

Change at work accelerates with multiple improvements to the context of work, carefully sequenced and timed within a short period. As long as the systems and its participants can absorb the change, the agenda for action should be constant and rigorous. A sense of urgency results and resistance diminishes because there is no chance of return to the status quo. In this manner, an organization gains the advantages of a crisis mentality. Just as a classroom can ready students for learning, changing how work gets done creates openings for application or reinforces application.

The basic work systems which can be altered to bring about the transformation of a firm or strategic business relationship are planning, business direction and monitoring performance, optimizing workflow and integrating information technology with other continuous improvements; communications, internal partnering relations and performance management—including reward and recognition; partnering relations in the value chain and financial engineering; and structure, which includes role expectations, teams, networks, and strategic units.

Most organizations accomplish change with single programs. Emphasis is on one aspect of work and then switches to a new program. The rate of change is typically 6 to 18 months. The failure of single-strike programs can be found in avoidance and imbalance. It is easy to avoid change if only one organization dynamic is affected. For example, management avoids offering training sessions on valuation models because priority meetings for the planning cycle are taking place. Then everyone wonders why no one can apply the valuation models in planning preparation.

Conflicting priorities become excuses to avoid change and learning. Imbalance occurs when one system receives too much attention. An illustration of this phenomenon is forcing a customer sales service unit to build an information system from scratch when an off-the-shelf program would suffice. The design from scratch is incomplete because of the work demands of those responsible for the design. This causes problems with customers, or in other situations, hinders compliance with regulators. In some cases, employee morale suffers.

Rarely is a holistic approach taken. A holistic approach is more than a point of integration. It involves methods for development and implementation. In the illustration above, a small task force of the customer sales service unit could assist in the design of the new information system or the group could use a war room with information technology (IT) specialists in tailoring a standard approach—further reducing the time required for their input. The holistic approach is a plan addressing what must be learned and changed first. As employees grasp the first changes, the company implements the next learnings. Each piece of the change effort is carefully fitted with the others for mutual reinforcement.

One good example of a holistic approach is introducing a planning system which aligns capital deployment and value performance with rewards. The emphasis goes to these major efforts, yet parallel work is done on elements of the major efforts: the bonus administrative framework gets a priority among human resource specialists. Information technology workers provide software for calculating value added for shareholders. They also take on the development of an integrated financial system over an extended period of months. Capital deployment decision making takes place in special meetings for the first year or two to promote learning in the new valuation process and collaborative methods—eventually settling into a more routine planning process. In this manner, concurrent and parallel work come together to create a mosaic for change. To be successful, holistic approaches of this nature are adaptive, able to react to new opportunity or constraints.

Double-Dipping, Double Exposure

In building strategic business relations today, time can be a precious commodity. The pressure stems from shorter and shorter life cycles, rapid deployment by imitators, strategic competitor incursions into your share, and the introduction of technology from allied fields which wholly disrupt the market. Accelerating learning is important to getting started, product launches, and expansion, particularly overseas.

Our learning discussion investigates next a different aspect of how we acquire knowledge. There are many methods for adult learning: life experience, lecture, reading, case study, templates, demonstration, simulation, coaching, mentoring, and exercises. The aim of learning can be simple awareness, understanding, or development of knowledge or a skill set for application. Carefully orchestrated, the learning can expedite grasping skill sets and competencies required for success.

It is useful to remember that we do not all catch on at the same time or with the same learning experience or with the same amount of investment in learning. The most effective learning takes planning and resources for multiple events reinforced by more than one method. In a very busy world, where time and resources are precious, a company needs another reinforcement—a clear endorsement by leadership and reward/recognition for results in application. This is why it is important for leaders to spend time interacting with employees to update, explain, and educate.

These actions reinforce written communication, announcements, and people's own perceptions of market news. What is critical is the opportunity to dialogue. Questions are answered, lessons are taught, and information is shared. In the richness of the interaction, the message gets across and is believed. The "ah-ha" reaction is more likely to spring from the dialogue than the initial lecture or discussion. The first pass on communication just opens the mind for consideration— it rarely achieves belief or acceptance.

Dialogue also includes a recognition element. The person feels special because the company invests time in his development. There are other benefits to leadership involvement. Leaders can learn what aspect of their message gets across and what does not. They can receive feedback known to employees through their networks beyond work. The feedback may enrich competitive intelligence. In this way, learning is a catalyst for gaining adaptive information about the market which might otherwise have been overlooked.

All learning processes occur in adaptive cognition. As we noted earlier, this is the interactive and simultaneous dynamic of sensing, thinking, and acting. Inherent to adaptive cognition is the social influence and stimulation of others. One person says something which cues another. As the conversation progresses, each gleans and records insights.

War rooms are places where leaders and staff post commercial, technological, financial, and orchestration issues (structure, learnings, communication) for review. War rooms are designed to address complex matters. They fully exploit adaptive cognition by promoting interactions and leveraging multimedia to serve as an artificial memory and induce fast-paced, involved human dynamics. Companies frequently use war rooms in planning alliances.

The format for learning need not always be linear. Learning can come and go. Effective learning may require experimentation in application and other reinforcement. Learning can interact with creativity, requiring nonlinear views to provide insight. Seeing the issue from a different angle or viewpoint, stepping out of a conventional paradigm, taking a systems view of causes and their interactions, and examining adaptations and their interdependencies are examples of nonlinear thinking. Most of us prefer to learn by progressing through basic material and advancing to more complex issues as we become more sophisticated.

There are many ways to learn and we do not all learn the same way. Multiple methods make sense because each experience reinforces our pattern of learning. Learning is less likely to escape us if we see the new information more than once and find utility for it in more than one context.

Repeated exposure is smart business. We typically need to progress across learning experiences to comprehend a subject fully. Think about how effective you would be jumping into derivatives if you did not grasp the basics of accounting and finance. You could misuse a technical financial term when selecting your derivative and end up assuming greater risk.

We increase our understanding by taking on basics first, then pursuing more complicated matters. Learning is an adaptive process. One concept can build on another. We may need to change what we learn on the basis of actual experience. We may have to refine and repair our learning.

Repeated exposure permits more time to think and reinforces and grants the chance to build on what we have learned. This may facilitate a superior understanding for application. We may improve the learning process itself by integrating the reality of the marketplace. This integration helps people make basic connections about how the concept becomes a reality. The early success encourages more attempts to apply the concept.

For most people in the workforce, learning is merely attendance at a seminar. Learning is actually much more dynamic. It is a part of every experience. Even so, a focused effort will accelerate learning and broaden impact. Individual styles of learning need to be understood by teachers and coaches so they can begin where learners truly are. This makes the effort to expand horizons easier.

By dedicating time to the subjects we need to know and drawing on the methods which work best for us—seminars, simulations, readings, conversations, interactive computing, whatever—learning will be more interesting and enjoyable. As leaders, we should do for others as we would do for ourselves. Adapt learning to current understanding, beliefs, and prior experience. Learning is low-hanging fruit to be picked in the harvest of shareholder value. Knowledge can be a function of opportunity and need. It should not merely serve the convenience of those delivering the learning.

Finally, shared learning among partners creates two advantages. First, the shared experience is an opportunity for informal team building. The common experience, with appropriate encouragement, can be an opportunity to learn about one another as well as be the "thing we did together." Second, the learning subject matter becomes the common, shared approach. "It is neither yours nor ours alone. It is ours together."

Mentoring—The Power in the "Gipper"

Mentoring began to get attention in the late 1970s as popular magazines and books talked about life stages. These works spoke about how important mentors are in the early progress of young people and how older workers have begun to value and enjoy mentoring. Through the 1980s mentoring gained in popularity with more emphasis on understanding career life. Formal programs evolved, in particular, as an effort within affirmative action. Then the value taken in mentoring hit rock bottom for several years while companies applied mentoring only for the highest levels in a firm. Firms were turning their backs on paternalism in organization style, and the preoccupation with downsizing and reengineering captured attention. Mentoring continued in informal ways.

In the 1990s, mentoring returned with the appreciation of how important it is to prepare people to grasp change and respond or learn new processes and new products. It is becoming an overused term, but this writing approaches the topic differently from most treatments.

From either the view of the individual to be taught or the firm sponsoring the learning companies should choose mentors with care. There are two dimensions to examining mentoring relationships: 1) how a firm sponsors knowledge development to sustain and enhance vitality, and 2) the nature of the actual mentoring relationship.

How and What Firms Sponsor to Build Knowledge

For matters of knowledge, the mentor's expertise should be well established. This, however, is not enough. The mentor should be a capable teacher and coach. These are interrelated, yet distinct, skill sets. Teachers are able to develop the curriculum and communicate in a manner fitting the learners' needs. Skills in lecturing, demonstration, curriculum development, lesson plans, evaluating learning, interactive computer learning, and visualization are important.

Coaching is more an application skill. The mentor may not be able to lecture and explain concepts but is expert at the task. The coach must possess subject matter expertise and the ability to provide timely and effective feedback to reinforce learning or refine application. A coach in the business setting is more concerned with the whole task of technology transfer.

A teacher in business is typically a seminar leader focused on a concept, a case study, and increasingly, a simulation exercise. His ability to go beyond a lesson plan and related briefs is limited. The teacher is event-oriented and supports the learning of all event participants. Some teachers can coach. In business, it is harder to merge the roles than in a schoolroom or university seminar.

The need for expertise and intimate presence is greater for a workplace coach. Coaching is an expensive investment. This is why many companies limit their learning offerings to seminars. The gap between seminar and application is also expensive. To their credit, some organizations have begun to teach managers to be coaches.

Coaches focus on a person's capability to achieve a result. In the beginning, coaching may be more intense than later in the mentoring process. The coach may do the task while the learner observes. As time passes, the learner takes more and more responsibility. Eventually, the learner is only observed. Then the learner solos—no observation. The role for the coach is to act as a sounding board in planning and assist with a debriefing to glean lessons for future applications. In time, the coach goes back to doing the work or coaches others. Periodically, the coach may assist in renewal; this would begin another cycle of development or shift emphasis to sustaining improvement. This is the cycle used in training pilots. It is very effective.

In the 1980s and continuing through today, the concept of train-the-trainer prepares coaches to be effective teachers. The gaps disrupting this strategy are:

- Too often the investment is in people of declining or little influence to operations. As a result, they get ignored and the learning is set aside in application.
- The training teaches people not to think through the application but simply to regurgitate the material proffered.
- One group designs materials, another prepares them, and a third group applies them. The chance for dilution increases with each step.

Two other limitations may afflict corporate training. These impair the quality of mentoring in knowledge development sponsored by firms. One is the intersection of the human touch and business analytics. These skills sets are not mutually exclusive. In entrepreneurship or general and senior management, the human touch and business analytics intersect frequently—albeit at different degrees of success. In the specialists' roles, few understanding the human touch have taken the time to understand more than the veneer of business value management.

For example, among human relations and learning specialists, you will find advocates for shareholder value add (SVA). They eagerly attend the training sessions on SVA. Ask them to calculate an application. Ask them what goes into consideration for an investment decision. Ask them to describe the business landscape in detail. Better yet, ask them to make a capital deployment recommendation and justify it. We have done so and been disappointed. They appear to be politicians echoing a campaign slogan for SVA, not businesspeople pursuing value with an effective tool. Their credibility as instructors is suspect.

A parallel illustration can be made among operations, technical, marketing, and financial specialists and managers. It is vogue to be concerned with how a company manages relationships. Inquire about what you look for in groups. The superficial observing skills are there. They know who influences and why; they realize who is passive and why. They even know how "to build" on one another's comments in the fray. What is missing?

They shrink group dynamics to narrow thinking by using traditional problem-solving tools which appear under new labels. True, these play a role. They help achieve focus quickly by narrowing the problem into a solution. Tactically, bringing forth a focus can be a catalyst for action. However, this may be good only for the moment.

The troubling aspect is that these same specialists similarly manage strategic discussions with narrow thinking. This plays out in more than one way. The managers may not value a difference in opinion and either suppress it or set it aside. They use a better vocabulary reflecting the process of human dynamics, but their behaviors have changed little. People leave the meeting with no ownership, and possibly with a bad taste for the effort, or feeling manipulated. In today's complexity, more roles sit at the table. Some participants are not prepared to contribute. Bizarrely, despite their ignorance, they have influence on the decision because of who they are, not what they know. The narrow-minded view is permitting hierarchy to determine action. In this case, the internal process values elite participation over responding to the market.

The New Corporate Paternalism— Sacrifice and You Will Be Rewarded

In the new corporate paternalism, here is how corporate leadership is heard. "Dear employee (now called associate), we are not responsible for your knowing what you need to do on the job. We will make learning available on our terms—time, amount, method, and preparation are our decisions. You will have to catch on to survive. If you bother to participate, we may recognize you, regardless of the value of what you say and do. We understand you must be in the room to feel involved. Though you are present, we reserve the right to ignore you because we already have made our choice and to listen to you would be distracting. By the way, this is for your own good. You see, you will have a piece of the reward only if we succeed in the marketplace. Most important, we will protect all of us from your being wrong."

Scary stuff, this is. Organizations translate the worst of contemporary parenting to create latch-key employees—not really neglected but not cared for either. Employees are free to do as they please until they fail or get caught. Worse yet, the absence of caring disenfranchises employees—meaning they experience abandonment and have feelings about it. How fulfilled and enthused is a mouse in a fur-lined mouse trap? Stylish, frustrated, angry—certainly not happy and self-initiating.

Meetings are highly complicated. Group dynamics are the intersection of numerous individual expectations. An in-depth appreciation of what is really influencing results is usually missing. Human ambitions, attraction, boundaries to define inclusion and exclusion, competencies, human communication as well as the subject matter for discussion are patched together in a crazy quilt of possible behavior. Looking too narrowly at human behavior can lead to mistakes. On the other hand, grasping all there is in group dynamics offers insight into outcomes and how they are realized.

Corporate Learning Dynamics—The Cure for Knowledge

Also missing is a full appreciation of learning. What is needed? How best to deliver the material to be learned? How to orchestrate application? Learning is a popular theme these days. The popularity creates a renewed interest in training, but it has not necessarily improved its use in business. Many firms sponsor nice retreats. The experience in them leads to good feelings, but knowledge and encouragement for application are often absent.

There are a few good centers of executive education. As time passes, they risk creating a rigidity in managing the business landscape. Quasi-academic models are dominant. Standards take hold but are outmoded by market forces before they are fully implemented. The problem is that standards are imposed on topics which are in flux.

Only optimization opportunities result from standards and uniform application. These topics are rarely the subject of executive education. Aspirants on the corporate ladder do not challenge this sort of executive education, though they are quick to comment or complain outside the sessions. It is expedient for one's career just to comply and not point out shortfalls. As a result, executive education may defy adaptation and discovery of what is next. This is a tragedy since executive education is an important portal to the business landscape.

With more and more delegation of decisions to business units and middle managers, there is concern that managers depreciate or dismiss new ideas because they perceive the powers that be as not supporting the idea. Either management must truly delegate decisions for running the business or communication and relations must improve to the point that misperceptions are eschewed. Delegation in name only, or taking responsibility but keeping a political eye up the hierarchy, only delays progress.

Now and in the twenty-first century, new ideas are essential to growth. In pursuing new ideas, customer intimacy, understanding your customers' needs and getting regular feedback, is the key to both learning about needs prompting new ideas or, once the idea is matured, getting an audience for the new idea. Securing business and growing it through introducing innovation require a rapport with the customer. The rapport must possess substance.

Do you think people who suppress ideas to avoid controversy within their firm will ever risk stepping out to build relations with customers? Customer intimacy is an uncertain situation at best. There is more uncertainty in partnering than in running an individual firm. If leaders build relationships, will the customers see the relations as genuine? It is doubtful if these same people cannot relate to those working for them. Or do you think relations will be strong enough with customers to introduce new ideas? It is difficult to believe it possible if the people establishing the relations have not built relations sufficient for convincing their own bosses.

While much gets said about human dynamics, little is understood and little meaningful action takes place. Again we get only the veneer. Corporate learning depends greatly on a senior management's sponsorship of a training plan and process. This means learning professionals must possess the business acumen they advocate for others. In a similar way, other business professionals need more than a superficial understanding of the psychology of work, group dynamics, and learning processes.

Building any competency is a shared responsibility of the individual and the firm. It involves personal and company time. It takes many different occasions for learning, ranging from seminars to conversations to reading. Competency means there is competence. The appearance of understanding is not enough. Successful experience is the desired result. Firms will not have good coaches and teachers until those with the human touch learn more about business acumen and vice versa. The world has changed, and learning practices must be transformed to keep pace. Specialists can support this transformation by infusing learning technologies and methods. To do more and earn improved credibility, they must themselves gain new knowledge and experience. The twenty-first century leader must have a renaissance profile chiseled by mentors who are accomplished in the art. Otherwise they chip away at value with concepts in place of technique.

The other major limitation impacting corporate-sponsored mentoring is the absence of preparation. This begins with society as a whole. For example, in white-collar work, poor preparation shows up in the inadequate English language skills of recent college graduates. Companies are having to invest in written and oral communication training to compensate for what high schools and universities failed to engender in their students.

In companies, the lack of preparation in company-sponsored mentoring is most obvious in two circumstances. One is on-the-job training (OJT). Still the dominant means of job training, OJT is rarely more than being put on the job to sink or swim. If orientation exists, it encompasses dry material on administration or operations: ethics in trading, safety, and other regulatory issues. We have witnessed too many multimedia shows followed by simple tests. Some written driver's license exams are more demanding in terms of learning and skills development. Mandated by regulators, these efforts lack quality—all that is required are attendance and completion of common sense-based tests until there is an incident. Then there is a flurry of activity to upgrade courses and, for a while, everyone from top to bottom is a student.

The other circumstance in which preparation is remiss is seminars. Firms expect two- and three-day experiences to change long-standing habits and beliefs. When the rarer investment of a couple of weeks is made, the investment is for an isolated episode. This is not sufficient to build understanding and change behavior on the job. Modules spaced out over time reinforce the value of the concept and provide forums for continuing dialogue among all those targeted to change. In contrast to the single seminar, sessions across time impact learning more positively. They provide continuous learning about changing technology, business conditions, and means for managing business relationships. For example, it takes a year or so for new terms and conditions to become popular in agreements between parties. This means innovation is moving rapidly among the leaders, probably in a matter of only one or two months in order for global change to happen in a year.

Academic degree programs like executive MBAs can be useful. Their limitations are that some faculty will not have the experience on which to base their coaching or quality will vary across subjects. One school may be strong in finance but weak or mediocre in human behavior at work.

Sometimes the executive encounters views or paradigms back on the job that are different from those in the classroom. It is not that one or the other is right; instead, one way to skin the cat needs to be chosen at some level to reduce confusion. Usually, it is more a matter of vocabulary than substantive differences in approach. Figuring out the best of both worlds may foster creativity. The task for the executive is then to bring the better approach forward to the attention of the firm. The alternative would happen when the MBA cirriculum is fully aligned with the firm. Of course, instructors in this case must be careful to avoid introducing rigidity by having a company-insulated curriculum. Striking the balance between outside and inside is an art where astute observation and judgment count. While corporate training is truly a creative process, most company curriculum or learning officers take the easy way out.

Some major corporations have attempted to replicate the learning center concept. Their standard is General Electric, which invested heavily in aligning change with learning and application. Few succeeded in doing little more than creating a mini-service center for seminars at lovely settings for random conversations and big events. Substance is missing in such learning centers more than it is present. Those charged with stewarding centers must be mindful they are a business within a business. They have an important mission: the learning agenda for the firm. Too many administrators recruit costly programs which raise their prestige among their circle of colleagues but do little to transform behavior for the firm. Many administrators, on the other hand, attempt to do too much internally. They absorb from the best but deliver with inexperienced trainers who mouth the words but cannot field real life scenarios or deviate from a script in simulations. For some administrators, the goal is more to protect the center than deliver what the firm requires. (We have never executed a simulation the same way twice because the choices made by participants and their real-life experiences have equal or greater meaning than the staid learning exercise.)

The answer is not to eliminate residential centers but to make them vital to the firm's market requirements. In a world of numerous programs, constantly changing needs, and virtual delivery by telecom or Internet, the use of the center should shift. Do not invest in seminars by the dozen and licensing trainers to mimic a trainer's manual. Send the firm's learners away to universities, professional organizations, and vendors who mix attendees across organizations. In this manner, people learn the material and build networks. Import a seminar when you must tailor proprietary knowledge such as the application of valuation models or account practices for market strategies.

The residential setting of a center has value as a place to conduct customer meetings, build a community spirit, do planning and lookback analyses, share learnings (best practices) from experiences, and conduct simulations. Centers are appropriate for optimization training—technical learnings and workflow improvement. Centers should be a catalyst for adaptation discussions and planning.

The test for a good trainer is in the simulation and Q&A portions of learning. Can they think on their feet and give substantive replies to participant inquiries? No one knows everything, but never having done the work is being too remiss. Minimally, potential trainers should have observed the business transactions first-hand. Instincts and insight are more a function of experience than reading books and articles. The credibility of an entire seminar can evaporate in the minds of participants because it comes off as academic or incomplete. (A few years ago, in a major energy concern, an instructor made an observation which just did not fit with our reality. We asked where the instructor learned the idea. It was from a movie. Inexperienced people with good presentation skills can be scary.)

Simulations have been with us for some time. The ancient Greeks and earlier peoples used simulations to anticipate battlefield events. In 1811 the Prussians used game boards to simulate battle. In 1887 the U.S. Naval War College began using war games in their curriculum.[2] Now we find simulations throughout the defense, intelligence, and law enforcement communities. Every summer the White House sponsors global games to ready situation room staff and advisors.

Simulations offer great value for bringing strategy alive and offering practice for application. Simulations pit teams, role-playing and operating in scenarios, against one another to complete a commercial venture. Simulations need to be simple yet must represent realistic views of the market. Too often simulations overplay group dynamics to the exclusion of what needs to be learned. Simulations are often prepared by corporate educators who do not know how the market functions. We corrected a client's case studies once to introduce how various financial engineering firms would compete against multinationals. The previous simulation only addressed going head-to-head with another strategic buyer. What good is a simulation which does not scope out all the players or educate on their means for judging or extracting value? One of the important opportunities in simulations is to experiment with newly learned approaches.

The trend by firms to offer more learning is encouraging. However, this trend does not fully deploy adult learning methods. Investments in brick and mortar with overhead staffs foster the creation of institutions, and thus more activity than results. The academic model is not viable for adaptive thinking, and it is the dominant model. Academic institutions are feudal systems—steeped in hierarchical control. Faculty obsessed with collegial recognition subordinate basics to fancy and teach rigid models in which adaptation to the market suffers.

Mentoring as a Kind of Business Relationship

Mentoring is one of the partnerships found in employment as well as within relationships between firms. Within firms, mentoring passes on from one generation to the next a skill, competence, or network. Though the generation difference often parallels chronological age, experience with the product or task may be the basis for the generation difference.

Between firms, the focus of mentoring is more likely a specific technology transfer related to a firm's product or a sharing of a customer network. The transfer is from firm to firm and not necessarily related to one generation of worker to another. Nonetheless, a knowledgeable person in one firm assists someone in the other firm in learning.

Mentoring can be one of the most intimate relationships in business. Mentors and learners share a great deal of time and a great deal of information about choices and why choices are made. The potential for intimacy reinforces the caution to be selective about mentors.

Mentors can often become close friends with their students. Strong loyalties can evolve and expectations for mutual support extend across time. The relationship can be limiting when feelings of obligation hold back progress so as not to be disloyal to a sponsor. This may happen when a former student aligns with a mentor because of loyalty instead of good business sense. Organizations must be watchful for inappropriate behavior. The intimacy can go beyond norms of the firm and the law.

Managers should watch for several forms of dysfunctional mentoring. Mentors may sponsor and protect their students, giving advantage in career climbs to the less qualified when better candidates for the opportunity exist. Loyalty can be manipulated to involve people in fraud. Mentors and learners may be pressured to cover up criminal activity. The relationship may also be exploited with an invitation to join into a scheme. Sexual liaisons are not unknown. Dominance can occur and talent be suppressed.

However, much more good comes from mentoring than bad. The process makes possible transfer of the most intricate and complicated technology. Mentoring is just as common a method for teaching simpler tasks which make up every sort of operation. Mentoring can accelerate and ensure the supervision of early application in operations.

The transfer of understanding inherent to mentoring makes possible progress across generations. Important technical and medical innovations can be passed down through generations. Institutions can leverage continuity when mentor and student end up in different places with different challenges. A common understanding permits a shared dialogue about diverse situations for the same challenge. The sharing creates overlap among intents which combine to yield innovation.

Mentoring is a function of good listening and coaching skills. Of equal importance is the subject matter expertise of the mentor. An appreciation for life and its consequences does not hurt. The mentor provides from time to time a frame of reference: "Yes, at this point in your career, your ambitions are normal," "You may want to consider how your choices are impacting home life so you make the choices with purpose," or "Here is what comes next in honing your expertise."

Part Two: What You Need to Learn about Partnering

Two fundamental skill sets define the learning context for partnering: human relations skills and partnering practices. As we said before, they are not discrete competencies. The ideal is to be strong in both. We describe them as independent for two reasons. The first is that most learn them as independent skill sets. The other is that the human relations skills can be applied across different settings and cultures. Partnering practices are more situation-dependent. They align to a particular step in the partnering process or to the kind of relationship to be established.

Those involved in partnering need to master the following competencies:

- Effective human relations in partnering: trust development, acceptance management, listening, expressing ideas, and learning
- Strategic business relations (SBR): prospecting, deal making, joint business planning, shared governance, and extracting value in successful operation

- Customer intimacy strategy
- Reality-based, data-based negotiation
- Merging cultures and work systems
- Supplier-customer action teams (SCATs) in value chains
- Management of shared operations

The means to acquire the partnering competencies in human relations are seminars, simulations, readings, and experiences ranging from selecting worthy partners and negotiation of deals to orchestrating start-up, operations and growth.

CIVILITY—THE GRACE IN THE 21ST CENTURY

Civility is a fluid dynamic important to change. Civility makes dialogue possible and promotes fair play. Partnering can inspire civility. Civility may facilitate strong relationships capable of partnering. As civility positions a relationship in a continuing dialogue, the content of the dialogue determines the merits of the relationship. The more civil the proceeding, the more the participants can tolerate confrontation. This fosters conflict resolution and creative, though at times loud, discussion. Of the four building blocks for trust, civility is as much an end as it is a means. A collection of good choices concerning fairness, respect, and honesty comprises civility.

In a state of civility, one can easily realize trust. Civility is a foundation or a solid platform in the architecture for trust. Civility makes possible a peace and comfort for the exchange of viewpoints. An air of tolerance results and at least invites listening. A dialogue to explore ideas and opinions is highly probable. A civil atmosphere makes possible the conversations essential for building trust.

In international commerce, civility is even more important in the early exchanges. Commerce is an extension of diplomacy in many lands. Imperialism is long over, but many societies still feel its imprint. Diplomacy is not civility. Being civil is part of diplomacy. Diplomacy is about sustaining communication. Diplomacy does not have to be fair or level-headed but does have to promote a continuing dialogue.

We already commented on the power of partnering to encourage the best in human behavior. There are a few reasons for civil conduct in partnerships. One is the human tendency to put one's best foot forward to "outsiders." As time together improves familiarity, you would expect the relationship to experience tensions. We believe it does, but other forces keep people at their best. One is that familiarity over time builds an intimacy and shared destiny. Teamwork should result.

Another reason for civil behavior in partnerships is closer scrutiny by more than one owner. The expectations of more than one owner yield a broader, if not more intense, review of a business: its workings, performance results, and plans for the future.

Joint endeavors with their multiple owners are less susceptible to hierarchical interference. That is, partnering tends to limit layers of management. Partners consider two or more owners engaged in stewardship as burdensome and they do not wish to increase overhead by adding additional tiers of management.

Information flows more freely in alliances or partnerships due to the flat structure and more frequent review. To the benefit of partnerships, collusion is not as easy to effect in a hierarchy composed of multiple career paths serving more than one owner. Loyalties are too fluid and mixed to promote the lasting cliques or gangs found in the bureaucracies of multinationals. Alliances do not eliminate good old girls' and boys' networks, but they sharply reduce threir influence.

Our advocacy for joint efforts needs qualification. An important interaction exists between civility and effective joint operation. Most executives, including those interviewed for this book and ones we have advised, do not perceive joint efforts as less cumbersome. The reason for the gap between their general experience and these remarks is the interaction of civility and multiple partners. Without civility, the advantages already mentioned do not accrue.

Civility is an atmosphere created by the prevailing norms of behavior in a community. In the marketplace, civility is the point at which the transfer of ownership preserves value to encourage lasting economic exchange. Buyers will be buyers again and again. Providers will find incentives to offer goods and services across time. These are truisms in free markets. As the world moves to greater freedom in trade, the obvious is too often forgotten. Exploitation is not unknown.

At a basic level of civility, the marketplace is safe for the conduct of business. Civility thwarts violence and theft. It preserves value by preventing destruction or removal without payment. The next level of civility prevents exploitation. People do not take advantage of each other. In part, they fear the tables might turn. They are willing to pay a fair value even when they could take advantage of the situation. A fair price is more likely to mean the maker of the product or the provider of the service will continue in her business. In the future, when a need again surfaces, her product or service will be available for purchase.

On the other hand, the provider asks a fair price. In this way, a customer can afford to purchase again and return in the future. The marketplace determines the meaning of fair price. A fair price pays back the investment, covers expenses, and yields a competitive return among capital projects.

Exploitation is a function of risking future purchases by taking too much. The marketplace also defines what is too much. Too much is a multiple of a fair profit. "Too much" erodes a customer base and encourages new entrants to pursue the pickings. New participants may lack an understanding of the industry and have no appreciation for standards of conduct, quality, or responsible care in delivery.

Civility at this level then is fairness and precludes exploitation. Few appreciate the ramifications of exploitation over the long haul.

The market grows fragile with the new entrants who hope to join in the exploitation. Eventually, a consolidation is needed to sustain a reasonable return and restore integrity to the industry. This is an arduous process and its opportunity cost outweighs the benefits of its catalyst—the short-run exploitation.

The Civil Thing to Do—Use Protection

Civility may provide an authority to enforce safety in the exchange of economic value. The authority may police against theft or impose rights to protect investment. An example of the latter is intellectual property protected by patents. The authority exists to protect investors and inventors and encourage them and others to support future invention and innovation.

In practice, some firms have abused these rights. This abuse brought about new legislation which is more refined and specific about economic performance. The objective is to trigger market forces and terminate protection when exploitation can be measured. This is not a new phenomenon for disputes presented in case law. What is new is the world's moving more and more into free trade. In part, this movement is the result of changing political realities opening new markets. Where political institutions are not changing, other forces are at play to induce free trade. The ease of transport, access to information about products and services, and the delivery of services made possible by the Internet all combine to compel freer trade.

It is likely that new laws and trade agreements will be more specific about a product or service in terms of its science, life cycle, and market-economic performance. In this manner, broad protection will erode as the product or property ages or loses its market value.

In the future, smart players will not hide behind protection and exploit. They will invest more often in worthy capital projects to innovate with customers. They will learn about their customers' needs. Customers will know about this potential and companies will seek customers' active participation in development. This strategy of customer intimacy will secure current business and build new and profitable growth.

Today the protected too frequently exploit the rights granted by civil authority. It is not uncommon to find that those who gather great profits through protection waste the excess profits. Whether the profit is wasted or not, the excessive profit-taking may choke their distribution channel and customers. Such firms keep prices high until the bitter end of protection and set themselves up for punishment when the authority removes the exclusive right.

Future protection becomes more difficult to earn as consumers force laws and trade agreements to eschew the opportunity for exploitation. The exploiting strategy invites revenge from the channel and customers. Customers and distributors abandon the exploiter or extract extraordinary concessions and commitments for him to regain acceptance. The cost of exploitation may also include exclusion from alliance opportunities in new growth. Uncivil conduct carries a high price in the long-term view.

Civility provides a means within the appropriate authority for resolving disputes, a means by which justice can be expected. Theft is prosecuted. Unfair deals are set straight, and restitution can be expected. The authority may be within a community or a state. At times the authority resides not in one body of government but in an agreement among them for trade. In trade agreements, access to future business— of the sort in dispute or in an entirely distinct industry—is the leverage to bring about enforcement among nations.

The Ballet in Civility

A more sophisticated level of civility offers much more. It is a place where civility means that participants can expect kindness, caring, and trust. It is an atmosphere of harmony. Curiously, in a harmonious environment, parties manage differences very differently from a contentious environment. They tolerate differences, if not encouraging, leveraging, or celebrating them.

War Story

From Sunsets to Mind Sets

One afternoon we were the luncheon guests of a prominent citizen of Santa Fe. Our hostess has the means to live anywhere in the world. In a life of travel and experience of humankind—good and bad—she chose Santa Fe as a home. We inquired as to her choice. Above the explanations of the natural beauty of mountains and desert, magnificent sunsets, casual elegance, or the sophisticated art culture typically offered as answers, our hostess expressed her greatest experience of Santa Fe. She enjoys the atmosphere of acceptance for all in humanity. People are permitted to be who they are without intrusion, evaluation, or discourtesy.

You can be anyone, anything, from anywhere and offer any opinion, and you will be tolerated, if not accepted. This is a celebration of individualism within a community collective.

This may sound like lines from the *Star Trek* shows. In reality, the *Star Trek* fiction is a fine metaphor. On the deck of various starships *Enterprise* for over 30 years, we watched creatures of all galaxies collaborate on a shared mission. Tensions among different cultures created plots of interest. In the end, resolution came from focusing on a common objective. At times, it was "us against them." Just as often, it was "us figuring out how to be us."

This is what you find in business partnerships. People from different disciplines representing different organizational cultures come together to pursue a shared responsibility for results. The plots are about making it work. The profits are the applause for good performance.

You can leverage differences as a catalyst for creativity. The willingness to tolerate blooms into a curiosity. Curiosity promotes exploration and many people offer ideas and opinions. The expression of ideas stimulates still other ideas. Often this intersection of two distinct thoughts produces new ideas.

War Story

The Bionic Cyber

We found at the Santa Fe Institute an immunologist and a computer scientist who carpooled for a few years. Over time they taught one another the tenets of their professional views of the world. They also taught and learned the other's vocabulary. Eventually the computer scientist began to think of her linear computer programming with organic, natural models. The result is a model for protecting computers from viruses based upon the nonlinear process that antibodies use to protect our bodies from disease. Different worlds intersected to create insight and redefine old paradigms. The messy, ugly duckling of a program emerged as a beautiful swan of cyber performance. Applause! Applause!

When Civility Is Missing in Action

Do not confuse civility with politeness that has an evil intent. Cruelty is cruelty, no matter the calm or elegance in which it is expressed. Some shallow people are skeptical about civil conduct in casual contact or at the outset of a relationship. We learn not to trust courtesy. This skepticism unnecessarily protracts the development of civility.

Most people can sense the reality of intent over time. Some guess at it right away. Varying levels of civility are available based on the judgment of intent. People search behavior to judge sincerity in the caring expressed. When caring proves to be genuine, acceptance is broad-based and trust is easily nurtured.

If sincerity is missing, people check next for professionalism. They question, whether this person will act according to professional standards because this is what it means to fulfill the role—regardless of how they feel about the other person. Here civility is a "time-of-day" type gesture done for any stranger. It is a gesture with little substance for building acceptance for an idea or venture. Trust is nonexistent, if not impaired.

Finally, fundamental civility will result if the person believes the other party will act to preserve a personal reputation. If this is the basis for civility, it cannot withstand much pressure before evaporating. Once the other party has what he feels he can get, he is gone.

Two major forces have diluted civility. One is the "me" orientation. Too consumed with self, many are not even aware they are not being civil. For the most part, polite society ignored these people and they never learned the fun in caring and being cared for. They often lack manners and are rude without purpose.

We experience this in the lazy waiter, the snide sales clerk, and the rude receptionist. Worse yet is the "plastic" response. This results from the second force in society to be blamed for the dilution of civility— sales training. The training focuses on the use of language without human intent. It is a facade engendered to placate for what should have been done or to capture your attention to close a transaction.

Intonation, the inability to express anything other than an insipid cliché of customer service, and twisted expressions on contorted faces belie the words expressed. We know when we are getting a line and not service. This can annoy and even infuriate.

Self-control is to our benefit in these situations. Our annoyance may please the tormentor. An uncivil response will reward us with further tension and either preclude or lengthen the time needed to achieve the desired result.

Outbursts may elicit a short-lived, compliant response. However, they forfeit the chance for educating and conveying the benefits of civility and full performance. Worse yet, they invite negative opinion from others in the market with whom you have to deal in the future. Though it may not be earned by the other party or may not be as immediately satisfying, self-control has more long-term benefit than beating the courtesy-dead of the "me" generation.

The Evil at Work

All that is evil in humankind is possible in a work setting, and all partnering in commerce is a work setting for someone. There are three evils which probably exist in all organizations: "bureaupathology," self-centeredness, and fraud. Each is vanquished by the union of transparency and civility.

"Bureaupathology" is a term coined more than 20 years ago to capture all that is diseased about traditional, large organizations. The behaviors included are indifference to customer needs, excessive delay due to work avoidance or redundancy, infighting among departments, the advancement of the incompetent, and a value placed on appearance over actual effort.

Large organizations do not have to behave in this manner. The design of enterprise units within a large system makes work meaningful at lower levels—in particular, middle management, where empire building is learned and first practiced. Transparency defeats bureaucracy by making it difficult to hide dysfunctional behavior or blame others for mistakes. The dialogue in civility prompts exchanges defeating those who would otherwise hide in isolation. In darkness, evil thrives.

Civility and transparency restrict the opportunity for **self-centeredness.** Transparency makes exploitation known; civility provides the discussion prompting corrective action. When a person is taking advantage for her own needs, the fastest way to correct the situation is to make it known. Informally, a person loses support—first among subordinates and peers, then eventually among mentors and career sponsors. In the end, the self-centeredness erodes authority or superiors take it away. The greater the transparency and the stronger the atmosphere of civility, the faster the decline of the self-centered.

How do the self-centered get ahead? Their best ploys are taking credit for the work of others, sacrificing long-term value for short-term results, controlling access to decision makers, restricting information to decision makers, undermining others' credibility, and building empires serving themselves, not shareholder value. These manipulations cannot withstand the scrutiny of transparency and civil discourse. Few career sponsors would choose to or will be able to protect a public display of self-centeredness. When self-centeredness is at the top, the investment community can correct the situation, and eventually they do. In either case there must be mechanisms to reveal what is taking place and the caring by owners and leaders to find out what really goes on in their organization.

In the past and today, business people fear that top-down intrusion erodes confidence and the credibility of the managers under review. When the inquiry is routine and understood to be a tool to engender organizational vitality, this erosion is less likely. What those at the top must do is focus on deviations from strategy, and abuses in conduct. If owners and upper management engage in Monday morning quarterbacking of strategy, their worst fears will be realized.

Periodic, intensive organization reviews or "owner audits" by third parties can effect good use of transparency and facilitate civil discourse about how to do better. They most certainly can end self-centeredness. Growing in popularity, these function as an ombuds mechanism without the limitations of second guessing and collusion typical to a single ombudsman.

Before leaving self-centeredness, it is important to point out another of its forms—ignorance. Ignorance is best dealt with by learning. Transparency motivates firms to address ignorance. Civility plays two roles in mediating ignorance. It creates the opportunity to surface it in dialogue and determine how to resolve it. The other role for civility is to make the ignorant aware of how their ignorance adversely affects partners and coworkers.

Fraud is deceit of any sort which destroys or steals value from an enterprise. You need accounts and controls to track the movement of value. However, there are limits to what accounting and finance can do. Deceitful people can corrupt audits and alter routine paperwork or reports. As noted earlier, transparency is a great fraud buster. The role of civility is in what gets done about fraud. Too often firms shy away from prosecution to avoid lawsuits. On the other hand, a civil enterprise shows respect for the people in the firm. There must be integrity to judge fairly and, where fault is found, to prosecute. Otherwise the system does not show respect for those who did what is right all along.

Most people want to work where they know those who do not deserve to be a member of the firm are dealt with. The convenience of not doing what is right to avoid the risk of litigation has a cost. Less scrupulous partners and employees may begin to test the system. Worse yet, the good people give up hope in the values of integrity and fair play. After all, they are the ones who must continue to associate with the undesirable and carry the extra burden they create.

Evil exists in organizations. Its base will grow when deceit can be hidden and no dialogue exists for revealing and resolving the evil. It is not so much that civility attacks evil; rather civility fills the empty voids evil thrives on. Civility then creates a vital process which keeps evil in check.

Weaving the Fabric of Civility

The civility we advocate is more than diplomatic dialogue though a firm may need diplomacy to launch civility. Civility begins with safety and courtesy. It grows with kindness and caring.

For you to pursue civility, you must be willing to set aside differences and explore solutions. You must withhold those actions which would take advantage of someone. Your hope is that a shared good offers the greater good—if not now, then over the long haul. Civility includes self-control to avoid exploitation. Civility keeps attraction in line with the norms of the firm and society. The pulse of civility is an openness to difference. At its heart is tolerance.

Tolerance envelopes coping with nuances in human behavior which irritate and anger. In a harmonious environment, caring addresses tensions and restores harmony. In the stressful moments required for the process of restoring harmony, civility should prevail. In civility, all sides see the need to explore, understand, ask for forgiveness, and forgive.

Civility sets the stage for a calm in which all parties share facts and opinions for persuasion, and if necessary, hear and offer apologies.

Inherent to civility is the knowledge that we all make mistakes. Forgiveness and getting on with life restore productivity. Civility gets us back to work. It creates an atmosphere for learning, sharing information, and working together.

Civility exists because those involved recognize that chaos and anarchy are the alternatives. It is not unheard of for a firm, relationship, or community simply to get fed up with abuses and exploitation. Then they turn in a backlash reaction to embrace civility.

Preserving a calm presents the opportunity to build a bridge and continue with your pursuits. Civility is the eye of the storm in complexity. Movement from civility can be in the direction of mutual destruction or progress to harmony. Civility is the defining moment for the best or worst of things to come.

The most basic acts of civility guarantee no success. They enable success to evolve in a relationship by sponsoring dialogue with minimal distraction. Trust is erected on civil conduct.

Constructing Civility in Partnerships

Civility evolves when transparency exists in partnering. Disclosure of intent, backgrounds, and interests facilitates communication. Beyond transparency, civility in a partnership involves self-control with a proactive display of fairness and honesty. Parties do not express anger or frustration in an offensive manner. This is not withholding hostile emotions but making them known in a way which opens the door for further discussion and discovery. Civility includes the demonstration of fair play and truthfulness. If the other party perceives they will be treated fairly, they are willing to risk dialogue and, possibly, a commitment of wealth.

Learning in advance of partnering should address basic human communication competencies in listening, using feedback, and applying multiple means in conjunction with repetition to reinforce expressed intent. Demonstrating the value of courtesy, fairness, and honesty in relationships builds an awareness for the benefits of strategic business relations. It educates deal makers on the ramifications of quick, opportunistic grabs for unfair advantage.

Understanding how events evolve is a more effective deterrent to temptation than policy or command. In business, the need to show results can overshadow compliance to written and expressed direction. The belief that the transgression will not be detected and the challenge inborn to deception sets the stage for subterfuge in business. This is the importance of realistic simulation in business education. It helps the naïve and easily swayed to envision outcomes of all sorts.

Civility respects confidential information. Direction as to when firms need confidentiality agreements and what they need to include in the agreements is beneficial in preparing for civility in partnering. Of equal use are discussions about basic values. These reveal how a party will probably treat others.

Old, established relations which have doubt embedded in them from bad histories may need confession of responsibility in transgressions to return value to the relationship. At a minimum, mutual admission of fault may be useful in getting things on track for planning the future.

Civility does not suddenly appear in partnering. Civility is a function of the values and behaviors of all parties. One side does not determine civility of the partnership. Each side declares only the intent of its own actions. Reputation greatly influences expectations for a party's civil conduct. Potential partners should address unfair remarks about past conduct. Whenever past conduct has been unfair, you can expect that the other party will closely scrutinize your early choices and statements. Each party may closely watch early discussions regardless of the history. Values build a gateway to civility which, in turn, governs access to value-add.

The Role of Civility in Trust

Civility is the foundation for trust. It is the beginning topic in discourse. The more advanced the civility, the faster trust may develop. Trust can exist without civility. Thus, trust is more appropriately called unconditional love, which parents often have for their children. Trust can also be found in the spark of tempers before conflict resolution, when belief in each other and caring once again take hold.

Civility offers order and authority to sustain order. Too rigid an authority constrains adaptation. Ideally, civility offers sufficient order so that an individual, team, firm, or community has an identity, but this order is not so restrictive that it precludes change or growth.

Civility moves quickly into the realm of trust as caring builds. A trusting soul is more often than not a civil person. A civil person typically demonstrates a capacity to trust and be trusted.

ENVISIONING THE BUSINESS LANDSCAPE— THE 21ST CENTURY VISTA

In the complexity of a global marketplace, the skill for the next century is to track, interpret, and shape a business landscape. The capability includes picking the business factors of greatest importance to value, determining the interplay among them, envisioning opportunity, and acting on the opportunity before it is obvious to others. This means the ability to anticipate and influence the direction of events and processes, some of which may be beyond your direct control.

There are three dynamics in envisioning a business landscape: creating a vision of the future, understanding the workings of the business landscape, and orchestrating continuous action on the landscape.

Creating a Vision

For nearly 20 years, we have invited clients to offer their vision of the future. We told them to think of themselves as the tour escort for the visit of a reporter from a major business magazine like *Business Week, Forbes,* or *Fortune.* The visit was to take place 3, 5, 10, or more years into the future. The tour of the firm would have a magical capability. If the reporter wanted to see all of the global assets of a firm in the same day, this was possible. If the reporter wanted to read a file or overhear a conversation without being detected, that would be possible. The tour was to be planned and orchestrated to reveal how much progress was made in the firm from now to a point in the future. Finally, we give our concluding instruction, as the lights are turned down, for the participants to close their eyes and envision meeting the reporter at the local airport.

After the lights are turned back on, we ask participants to report what they saw and experienced. The facilitator captures their ideas and opinions with words, pictographs, and icons on a huge sheet of paper covering a wall. Without exception, this exercise brings forth creative insight into interpersonal relations, meaningful involvement in the partnership, application of technology—new and not yet invented, environmental improvement, new business opportunity, and more.

Descriptions of visions are often lively and detailed. Many offer insight into personal ambitions or reveal how caring people are. These discussions are valuable in defining shared interests. In one application among prospective partners, the vision expressed what had previously gone unsaid in earlier discussions. That is, heretofore the partners had voiced controversial, common interests. The freedom inherent in the exercise made risk-taking less risky among prospective partners. Once it became clear there were overlapping interests, excitement for partnering built.

There is not always agreement in a vision exercise, and different viewpoints occur side by side. Later, parties can use the information to refine strategies. Sometimes the difference stimulates creativity. At this gross level of discourse, the exercise is more a menu of possibilities. In possibility, there is hope.

Hope is a powerful influence in firms and their alliances. Its absence elicits bureaupathologies and indifference to performance. Hope inspires hard work and positive thinking about how to make something important happen.

As this exercise became more popular, many visions evolved into epistles for investor relations and employee communication. The insights were valuable but too rough, vague, overly lofty in nature, and otherwise not suitable for publication. The unbridled curiosity and creativity inherent to such discussion was edited to near perfect direction statements. Those directly involved in the editing possessed high ownership for the words and their meaning. Interpretation was difficult for those not present at the discussion. Instead of extending the process across a partnership, or up and down a hierarchy, a special group, nearly always at the top of the organization, crafted the vision into stone.

War Story

The Chairman's Manifesto

We were doing work in a Fortune 200 company several years after the trend in which firms professed their mission and vision in slick formats. Our task was to assist the board and senior management in diffusing their strategy to the investment community and employees around the world. As we entered the lobby, we noticed a competition for best quality poster. Dozens were displayed in the corporate headquarters lobby. At lunch we complimented the chairman on the contest, noting the recognition for contributors. Later in the lunchtime discussion, we were asked what was the biggest mistake a company could ever make in developing mission and vision statements.

We replied, "Carving them into stone—the most well-thought-out strategic intent may need to adapt. The more rigid in appearance, the less likely people are to feel responsible for thinking about adaptation or emerging with something new."

Our hosts were silent. Seldom do we impact a firm so strongly they are without words, so we inquired. It seems the chairman had the mission and vision carved into marble in the lobby.

A quality poster just happened to be covering them. We added, "Well, marble—that is a different matter from carving into everyday stone, but is it a sign of empowerment in the organization that people felt free to cover the statements with posters. Or have the statements grown stale and there is no concern that hanging posters over them would be taken as offensive?"

More importantly, when asked about hope, the management replied there was little found in the carving. Surprisingly, we were invited back for more work.

Despite the devolution in vision discussions, they continue to provide value to managing a business landscape. Visions are rough, vague, and constantly being adapted. They are powerful tools for shaping choices and defining hope. Visions are springboards to articulating goals and offering hope. Hope is a potent motivator. Management can base strategies on the choices made in talking through the common ground in visions. Visions invite people to action and begin the process of arriving at a focus for effort. The inset, "Guiding a Vision Exercise," provides ideas about prevision briefings and gives prompts for facilitating visioning exercises.

Guiding a Vision Exercise

Vision Prompts

- Focus and clarity of mission
- Opportunities to be realized
- Use of technology (especially information technology)
- Innovative financial engineering
- Customer intimacy
- Virtual value chain services
- Career dynamics (includes role clarification)
- Reward and recognition . . . celebration
- Owner interactions
- Owner involvement in alliance operation
- Future evolution of alliances
- Competitor benchmarking
- Competition leverage
- Organization dynamics of alliance: structure, communication, relationships, roles
- Exits and associated returns
- Envision 3, 5, 10 years into future (If more than one time frame is used, repeat the recording of thoughts in a like manner. This will make it less confusing and shape an evolution.)

Originally, facilitators saw visioning as a tool best used with a clean slate. That is, they led the vision exercise without exposure to any awareness of what innovations were available, a broad understanding of where the business was as the vision was shaped, or a discussion of how the vision would test into reality (and evolve in a manner so as to not overwhelm). The concern was that participants would see these factors as manipulation that would contaminate ownership for the vision.

As the practice of visioning became more routine, instructors gave briefings on what might be done and on possibilities for the technique in commerce, finance, organization, and technology. Surprisingly, ownership improved. Participants were less frustrated about knowledge which was missing. The reflective discussion on the vision contained less doubt that there would be support for innovation. The quality of the vision improved. People did their best to build on and express the insight of the briefing. The discussions about the process for "making it happen" were practical and filled with energy. Resistance and risk were less a concern.

Listed in the inset are potential briefing topics to be used depending on the audience. We recommend using all the briefing topics to stir thinking, yet simply passing these concepts out without briefing promotes thinking ahead of time. In the visioning meeting itself, facilitators will need to repeat the prompts. They should wait until after they have had a chance to remember participants on their own without being prompted. There can be a pregnant pause just before a deluge of comment comes from participants.

Understanding the Business Landscape

The second dynamic to envisioning a business landscape is understanding what makes up the landscape and gluing these pieces together.

A business landscape reveals an array of influences on value: investor relations, value chain optimization, financial engineering, direction and growth plans, learning systems, orchestration of actions, partnering relationships, and technology. Some influences are optimized against diminishing returns; others will emerge to set the patterns for increasing returns. If the firm succeeds, the patterns nourish the vision. Then the firm gains value.

Comprehending a business landscape can be overwhelming. There are numerous factors to consider in a swirl of interactions. Nonlinear thought processes are useful, but nonlinear views of the world are rare. Most learning follows a straight-line logic, e.g., accounting, finance, banking, engineering, law, computer science. In the sciences of biology and medicine, however, natural or organic models are more prevalent. The application in business of organic views requires a new understanding of the familiar.

We all try to reduce complex human behavior and nature to simple cause-effect statements. These are easier for us to describe in language. It helps us avoid the hard work of addressing complexity. To leverage fully the knowledge in a business landscape, we must think differently.

A systems view of the world and its events offers a way of seeing the interrelationships and interdependencies present in a business landscape. Much like a small boat at sea, the fate of the passengers is a function of what happens above and below the water's surface and the atmospheric forces in the sky. The systems of nature converge in a storm of possibilities. The moisture in the air is a function of the heat and the sea. Pressures in air like moisture and temperature create winds. Winds create waves. The pressure of one wave creates another. Undersea seismic activity creates yet other waves from a different direction.

The temptation is to focus solely on rowing the boat. That activity is mechanical power in action and feels right. Nonetheless, the limitation of this view is that the sea and the wind can carry the boat far to the side of the vector intended by rowing. Setting a course which adapts to surrounding conditions in the progress of the voyage determines success or failure.

A knack for seeing the interaction among influences is important to grasping a business landscape fully. The first step is sorting out all the possible influences and being open to the identification of still more influences as time passes. The next step is viewing events in the world as having multiple causes and admitting that one influence can affect another. Calibrating the impact of one influence on others then becomes important for understanding how a pattern may emerge. The objective is to see which are forcing adaptation and which are adapting or resisting.

You need to observe dominant forces for the magnitude of their influence on other factors, their mutation or integration with other forces, the pace of their movement in the business landscape, the rate of growth or devolution, and the breadth of their effect on the business landscape. As a pattern grows stronger and stronger, its effect will broaden to new horizons, forging more adaptation.

Understanding the pattern evolves in time to prediction. Prediction unlocks the secrets to value creation. Figuring out what to do, and when to do it, can be value-added knowledge.

A case illustration in Figures 4-1 through 4-3 representing a composite of firms in a business landscape clarifies meaning for the concept: envisioning the business landscape. The figures provide progressively more general conclusions. Figure 4-1 is a business "trellis" for a distribution partnership for a major energy concern.

LEVEL(S) CATEGORY BUSINESS MODEL / LEVER(S)	IMPACT TO SVA*	IMPACT TO GROWTH	MATERIALITY	LEVEL(S) IMPACTED
BUSINESS PLANNING	0	0	0	MEGA
VENTURE HUNTING	0	0	0	MEGA-MACRO
FINANCING	0	0	0	MEGA
BUSINESS MIX	0	0	0	MICRO-NANO
COMPETITIVE RESPONSE	0	0	0	MICRO-NANO
DISTRIBUTION	0	0	0	MEGA-MACRO
"PARTNER" FIT	0	0	0	MEGA-NANO
STEWARDSHIP AND GUIDANCE	0	0	0	MEGA
TRANSFORMATION	0	0	0	MEGA-NANO
PARTICIPATION	0	0	0	MEGA
ALIGNMENT TO FIRM	0	0	0	MEGA
FIRM CAPABILITY INFUSION	0	0	0	MEGA-NANO
FINANCIAL STRUCTURE	0	0	0	MEGA-MACRO
ORGANIZATION DESIGN	0	0	0	MEGA-NANO
LEGAL AGREEMENTS	0	0	0	MEGA-MACRO
AUTHORITIES AND RESPONSIBILITIES	0	0	0	MACRO-NANO
ACCOUNTS AND CONTROLS	0	0	0	MACRO-MICRO
STRATEGY IMPLEMENTATION	0	0	0	MICRO-NANO
BUSINESS COMMUNICATION	0	0	0	MICRO
TALENT, COMPETENCIES AND MOTIVATION	0	0	0	MEGA-MICRO
TECHNOLOGY TRANSFER: BEST PRACTICES	0	0	0	MEGA-MICRO
ENTREPRENEURSHIP	0	0	0	MEGA-NANO
INFRASTRUCTURE DEVELOPMENT	0	0	0	MICRO
OPTIMIZATION	0	0	0	MICRO-NANO

*SVA = SHAREHOLDER VALUE-ADDED

Figure 4-1. *The business landscape: a trellis of value interdependencies.*

The trellis defines the most important influences on value as represented by shareholder value-add, growth, and materiality (net income and market share). The trellis reveals the level in the relationship which is impacted. In the real display of the trellis, the magnitude of the relationship was measured. Certain factors had more influence on outcomes than others. They could be found anywhere: within the business model, among investor relations, within the governance process, and in portfolio management. The patterns within these dynamics indicated where the firm needed resources to improve performance.

Figure 4-2 represents ways to examine key interactions in a trellis. It is used to draft a business model, identify patterns, and grasp the interrelationships among actions and functions.

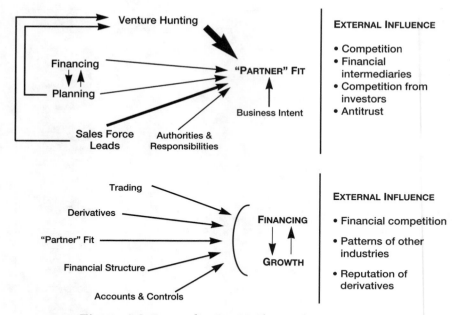

Figure 4-2. Immediate critical interdependencies.

In Figure 4-2, for example, sales force leads had significant impact on getting the right partner. The sales force knows who the performers are and how best to approach them. The design of the new organization had to address feedback from the sales force to deal makers. As venture hunting became better understood, the importance of the sales force advanced.

Figure 4-3 is the business model. This further reduces the complexity from the trellis to areas for action planning. The model also provides management a consistent view of performance.

Figure 4-3 clearly shows what is working, what is not working, and what is missing. You can see the impact any factor has on value and what warrants an appropriate action. As you make improvements, those factors that were reducing value will now become either catalysts or additives.

Orchestrating in the Business Landscape

The third dynamic in envisioning a business landscape is orchestrating continuous action. As noted above, as you study the land-

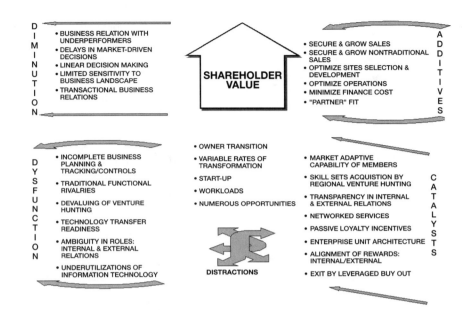

Figure 4-3. *Business model.*

scape, you will see patterns which indicate action to take. There are many more degrees of freedom to orchestration than most organizations choose to apply. Given the complexity of enterprises and the difficulty facing their ventures, more organizations should invest in better planning and development.

Any major change reflects myriad agendas: awareness building, design and development, orientation, communication, learning of skill sets and competencies, marketing and advertising, regulatory compliance, planning and execution of product launches, logistical support, feedback, sponsorship, stewardship, lookback analysis and strategy review, and continuous improvement or innovation. Together these agendas comprise performance in the marketplace.

The pace of change, the amount of change workers must absorb, and persistence in the change can all be measured, monitored, and influenced. Multiple methods and multiple exposures ensure creating a new reality. Each effort takes time and can serve to help or dilute effort. The primary tasks of orchestration are imagination, time management, and follow-through.

Consider now how you manage orchestration. Each action will have players. Every player has a career agenda. Orchestration must align actions to performance. You will need to track actions. You need to understand all of the above steps in terms of how they affect the others and are changed by them.

Trust and Envisioning the Business Landscape

Envisioning a business landscape is much like farming. Everything on the landscape is alive. Every day the landscape requires nourishment. Every life form is growing, adapting, and evolving. You must manage this parade of life. The farmer must see it all in his head, comprehend its meaning, set a direction, and be responsive to change. This is a creative act—drawing new useful inferences about what she can successfully grow and harvest. This is a visionary act—it is seeing the wave of the future and determining how to ride it. Understanding how everything fits together and orchestrating it all in the time available within a growing season are complex tasks. Business has its own planting and harvest. The business leadership challenge is to make the vision inviting to others so they will join in the effort of making things grow. In growth, there is hope and high potential for reward.

Building trust is more than a feeling. It is a tangible plan to make something happen. The feelings and claims about what will be invite others to join. Accomplishment sustains interest in the drive to the vision over time. Making something happen validates trust and invites trust in the next repetition of a business cycle or the next pursuit across the business landscape.

REFERENCES

1. William E. Halal, "Organizational Intelligence: What Is It and How Can Managers Use It," *Strategy & Business,* the newsletter for Booz Allen Hamilton, 4Q97, p. 1.

2. John E. Treat, George E. Thibarlt, and Amy Asin, "Dynamic Competitive Simulation: Wargaming as a Strategic Tool," *Strategy & Business,* the newsletter for Booz Allen Hamilton, 2Q96, p. 2–6.

CHAPTER 5

The Complexity Complex

GAY PARIS!

Complexity is like driving in Paris. At first it is sheer terror and agony. One moment you fear you will collide in the turbulence, the next you are certain you will never move again. You sit on the edge of your seat. As you adapt, you realize you can survive. You become one with the Parisians and drive as necessary. You begin to unwind along the ancient roads and approach Notre Dame.

Then it dawns on you—this is Paris. The beauty, romance, and history create an ambiance to engulf you. A pattern of charm dominates your view of the experience. How do you set a value on the moment?

Complexity frustrates, then engulfs you with challenge and insight. The essence of complexity is complication and intricacy. This vantage point intrigues some and challenges others. Most want to avoid complexity. Addressing complexity, by contrast, opens the door to value. Tunneling through complexity permits optimization, saving value. Weaving patterns builds new value.

Complexity recognizes that all things are interlocked in such a manner that it is difficult to determine what will happen. You need to know the direction of each element composing the complexity as well as how elements impact one another—do they combine, do they destroy one another in whole or in part, do they remain untouched, or do they function as catalysts and create something altogether different? In this chapter, we examine the complexity first on a human basis, and secondly, we explore how we as humans come together in business.

The stepping off point for discussion is the human landscape. This is what each of us faces at work and in our commercial transactions. It is the total of all human interaction in concert with each person's propensity for trust and career. The human landscape captures our positions, how they interlock with others in our firm, and how all those expectations link to partners.

The discussion moves next to the business landscape, the complexity surrounding a firm. Finance, operations, technology, and marketing realities combine with the human landscape. We then look at the interaction and covariance among all elements pertinent to value. This viewpoint helps explain why it is important in business performances to track interactions.

The final topic is about complexity as an economic phenomenon. We define and illustrate the meaning of intricate business dealings. In all, the review sounds pedantic. In reality, it is less pedantic and more about grasping the background that markets create for the business landscapes of firms. You will see the economic value inherent to complexity and the fundamentals for managing complexity in value creation. To envision why applying complexity concepts to business is a departure from conventional management, we illustrate with a composite of several companies. The illustration is a function of the pattern these firms succumbed to in the past. Some of the firms in the composite are beginning to emerge from the pattern set by the globalization of their respective industries. The illustration portrays the composite as a fictitious company in a 50-year transformation from the modern industrial age to today's nascent state of the knowledge era (we warned you it would sound pedantic).

THE HUMAN LANDSCAPE

Everyone brings to work expectations for themselves, expectations for others, and the expectations of others for them. These shape a human landscape of what can be done. In the 1970s Clay Alderfer at Yale University led a powerful exercise on reflecting on expectations. Here is how we have modified it over the years for partnering (see inset, "Expectations Exercise," on page 122).

Expectations Exercise

Place a dot at the center of a poster board to represent you.

Take a blue marker and place a dot to represent each of the individuals, teams, or units with whom you interface. Place the dots closer to the dot representing you if the interface is important. Circle the dots in red if the interface is frequent. Like connecting the dots in a game, linking the circles reveals key relationships.

Take a purple marker and do the same for people important to you in your home life. Some are likely to impact your business decision making.

Take a green marker and do the same for your partnering relationships outside the firm. Be complete—value chain partners, customers, investors, regulators, any venue you have external to the firm.

Take an orange marker and indicate where expectations anywhere on the paper are in conflict.

Reflect on what you have produced:

- How many relationships are there?
- Which are most important and why?
- How do you resolve conflicts among expectations?

Figure 5-1 shows the expectations a colleague experienced in a recent project and illustrates how involved expectations are. She followed the directions of the expectations exercise and listed interfaces with indications of their importance and turbulence, if any. Examine the figure and you find, in reference to a single client, the colleague has two dozen interfaces to manage. At the moment, two high-frequency relations experience some form of conflict (team leader and other clients). Two other relations are in conflict as well (niece and husband).

The complexity is high for everyone engaged in business. Dozens of people, each having expectations, impose their needs and wants on us. Some we respond to, others we resist, and still others we avoid. Many of these people influence decisions in our realm of work about value.

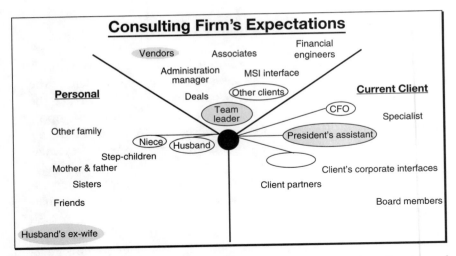

Figure 5-1. Case illustration of the expectations exercise. Ovals and shading indicate increased importance and conflict.

Boundaries—Complexity Wrapping or Psalms of Permeability

To cope with the complexity inherent in the flood of expectations, we set boundaries around ourselves. The boundaries reduce complexity to manageable categories of observation or choices. The boundaries help us work on the expectations, set them aside, or stage for a fight.

Different from avoiding an expectation, the fight is an aggressive stance to dismiss the relevance of the expectation, to decline involvement with those expressing the expectation, or to deny responsibility for the imposed expectation. On the other hand, we can set boundaries to encourage sharing and cooperation to work on the expectations. In this case, boundaries are permeable and permit energy, resources, and ideas to flow readily to others. Permeability relates to adaptation rather than avoidance or resistance.

Knowing how you manage your own boundaries and how your prospective partners, current partners, and other key interfaces manage their boundaries is important to value. The knowledge permits you to calibrate relationships and determine how best to approach the other party. The knowledge can even serve to pinpoint an approach to a specific transaction, e.g., negotiation, working out a solution for an operational issue, or resolving a conflict.

Alderfer introduced us to a useful way to assess boundaries that people and organizations create. His insight was applied to a wide variety of group dynamics and organization theory, most notably the work of Rioch and the Tavistock Institute. Here is how we adapted Alderfer's work over the years.

There are three basic states of boundaries, each having a different degree of permeability. Permeability is the extent to which information, energy, and resources may pass through the boundary. Boundaries can be overbound, ideal, or underbound (see Figure 5-2).

Very conservative individuals and groups tend to be **overbound**. They permit little in but can be very active at trying to persuade others. They leverage their strong internal agreement to press a message outward. As a result, their message flows out of the boundary with vigor. However, information from others is stymied. Without a "Radio-Free-Europe"-like intrusion, overbound groups have only their own doctrine. Neo-Nazi skinheads would be an example of a group prone to try persuading others but not open to information from those who are not aligned with their views.

Ideal boundaries are permeable, yet they sustain an identity and intent. They leverage conflict in two ways. One is that ideal groups capture creativity gained in the clash and integration of different viewpoints. The other is that ideal groups invite free and open debate to engender ownership through active participation in decision making. Ideal groups tolerate differences internally and with other parties. They are quick to adapt and operate in complexity at the edge of

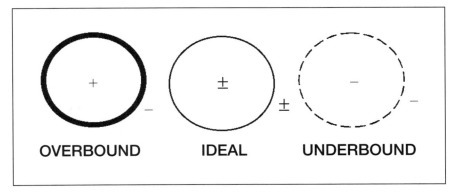

Figure 5-2. Permeability levels of boundaries.

overbound rigidity and the turbulence in underbound groups. They adapt, but do so within the principles of their intent as a group. For example, The March of Dimes was originally focused on eradicating polio from the lives of American children. With this accomplished, they changed their focus to birth defects, with the same intent of eradicating a serious, crippling disease from the lives of children.

Underbound individuals or groups are so loose about permitting information, energy, and resources to flow in and out, they are almost at risk of having no identity. Underbound groups waffle back and forth. In doing so, they perplex others about their true intent. Besides being together as a group, the purpose for partnering or collaborating may be unclear.

For example, the Clinton administration, in the last half of its first term, was criticized for not having a definable theme or direction. They declared positions on issues on an ad hoc basis. Collectively, no policy mosaic resulted, and critics noted inconsistencies among positions. Critics claim the motivation underlying their initiatives was a need to be accepted in public opinion polls. Clinton supporters claimed the responsiveness to opinion polls was a form of customer responsiveness, warranting adaptation. Which is true? What must be judged is the relationship between flexibility and the meaning or intent of the group. Flexibility at one level may be attempting to achieve the ideal boundary. At first the ad hoc nature of the ideal state can come across as the waffling seen in underbound groups. Adaptation can cause basic practices to be abandoned in favor of actions never before considered. Some see this as inconsistency.

In the beginning, it is hard to tell the difference between flexibility for adaptation and flexibility devolving into waffling. In the ideal state, though, there must be an intent for the group that everyone, inside or outside, can discern as the direction of the group. Image cannot supplant principles and philosophies which evidence the character and demeanor of an ideal group. Either the group is adapting appropriately to the world according to the theme of its intent or it is wandering about like a group of teenagers in a shopping mall. They are a group, but their course is a matter of immediate gratification or whimsy. There is no purpose to being a group per se, but the teens may, nonetheless, identify with the group. It is important to realize the strength in image. The identification with the group can be so strong, that they sport their colors and see themselves as a gang.

Table 5-1 shows boundary characteristics for different life circumstances. This list helps us diagnose the nature of a personal landscape or reveals the personification of a group of individuals. The diagnosis then offers insight as to how best to relate to others. In many cases, this knowledge gives an advantage in negotiations or offers understanding for partner behaviors.

War Story

A Tiger Cannot Change Its Spots

Some have difficulty with the concept of boundary. They want to pigeonhole a firm in one condition or the other. In reality, firms move along an array of characteristics denoting overbound, underbound, and ideal boundary status. Take, for instance, Exxon in the late 1970s. The corporate culture was generally described as overbound, but its expansion into diversified enterprises was underbound.

This one dimension of Exxon was very different from the rest of the company. The enterprises group was charged with pursuing growth, and this unwound into growth for growth's sake. Competencies did not drive acquisition decisions. The strategic intent was ill conceived and poorly defined: high-tech bicycle frames, computer components, solar energy, word processors, telecom devices, electric motors, golf clubs, and so on.

Control switched from centralized to decentralized and not in any pattern that made sense. The company applied then high-margin oil industry overhead salaries and structures inappropriately to narrow-margin businesses.

The incredible wealth of Exxon permitted numerous large purchases. Eventually the enterprise group evaluated economic performance and an exit from the enterprise businesses followed. The overbound functions of the firm took hold again. The short-term view of the enterprise businesses and the looming threat of declining price in the base business, oil, defeated attempts to mediate to an ideal state .

Table 5-1
Boundary Characteristics

Boundary dynamics	Overbound	Ideally bound	Underbound
Customer relations	Transactional	Intimate	Turbulent
Interest in diminishing returns	Obsesses	Optimizes	Forgets
Interest in increasing returns	Values exploitation	Sets patterns for growth and captures trends for own use	Rides trends se by others
Communication	Restricted	Open	Networked by cliques
Use of information	Withheld	Shared	Confused
Cooperation	Inside only	In-/outside	Fragmented
Conflict	Suppressed	Resolved	Ignited
Planning	Overkill	Business-directed	Fights fires
Control	Rigid	Flexible	Things fall into cracks
Resources	Afraid will lose	Full use	In danger of losing
Contribution	Individual	Individual and team	Crowd behavior
Responsiveness	Resists	Proactive	Overreacts
Mission	Fixed	Clear yet adapting	Unclear/no priority
Responsibility	Held by few	Participative	Dispersed
Change	Fights	Leverages	Does for the sake of changing
Respect	Power-based	Mutual	Barely exists

Boundaries are not fixed and can shift depending upon who is part of the event. Accordingly, the permeability adapts to the circumstance. The challenge is to adapt and use the knowledge in relationships. Typically, what you observe as dominant characteristics will not change much unless there is a crisis or a very purposeful effort to change.

Consider three scenarios to illustrate how you can use knowledge of boundary permeability to shape partnering effectiveness:

Scenario 1

Your own corporate organization is in disarray, but your product group feels there is an important growth deal to be made. You attribute the disarray to a spin-off the board and senior management are orchestrating. They do not want to upset the applecart with the Securities and Exchange Commission or the Federal Trade Commission.

You categorize your organization as predominantly underbound except at the very top. There the group is overbound. They withhold information, cooperation is only internal to the group, they are rigid about the decision to suspend all growth activity until the spin-off is complete, and they hold all the power.

Your product group is ideal in its boundaries. You share information, the time invested in the growth plan is not overdone, the group has a reputation for cooperating with others—no one in corporate perceives the group as likely to risk disrupting the spin-off. The group is looking for a way to adapt to the constraint of the spin-off.

How does a boundary assessment help determine what to do? First, the probability of gaining corporate acceptance is low. If there are better uses of time and the growth is not critical, the assessment indicates it is smarter to use time elsewhere on the business agenda. Second, if the growth play is critical, it will be critical to find the right opportunity to persuade upper management. A sponsor in that group will be essential for your argument to be heard where it counts.

A sponsor can provide insulation for risk takers at lower levels. Your ability to share information may make it comfortable to ask the prospective partner to help. They may have linkages to the top of your organization or be willing to earn a provisional approval from regulators to go ahead. Working their own interest satisfies your need to move forward. You will need to communicate to the sponsor how to relay information to your prospective partner. An external report of such activity to an overbound upper management would probably be a setback. Even if unsuccessful, senior management will admire you. Unlike your underbound counterparts, you pursued progress and demonstrated creativity.

Scenario 2

You judge a prospective partner to be primarily overbound, but the company shows key characteristics of other boundary conditions. Power is highly centralized despite the public image asserted. Reports to analysts and annual reports claim that the company delegates decision making to enterprise units. You have heard from others and watched yourself as the ad hoc manner in which the company manages capital deployment above the $20-million range repeatedly frustrates your peer, the global product CEO. In a corporation with sales over $6 billion, and a global product unit with sales of $700 million, this seems incoherent.

Cooperation is best inside the prospective partner. They are known to look out for themselves if times get tough; there is a history of quickly abandoning partners. If the firm were not wealthy, you are not sure it would still be in business. There is more crowd behavior than excellence in management and contribution. Their corporate group is very concerned about doing anything risky. Performance is off, and they do not want to jeopardize net worth in any way. However, this concern does not keep them from doing deals; they just take a long time, as laborious plans and reviews take place.

The global business unit possesses a critical technology. It could be an important component to your product, a new electronic platform. There are alternatives, but efficiency and performance for customers are not nearly as good.

What do you do according to this boundary assessment? The other side is overbound; they will probably be more receptive to the overture from a peer. Look for or establish a link at the board or senior management level to network a relationship aimed at your deal. If there is none to be leveraged, poll your senior management for a link. You may need to use accountants, bankers, lawyers, or supplier/customer leadership to effect an introduction. Keep your peer informed of your senior-level initiative, but do not share the details. More importantly, do not give the information in a manner which implies the peer can end the initiative above you.

Overbound systems do not promote risk takers in the climate described above nor do they give risk takers much attention or maneuvering room. Helping your peers look good by permitting them to prepare for the overture or tip off their senior level is a different matter. As best you can, keep the overture within the peer's framework for acceptance. This will make it easier for the prospective partner to align internally.

Find a way to alleviate the corporate office's concern about risk. Have your senior-level representative suggest either a license agreement for the technology or a joint venture which is structured to minimize risk. This way, the prospective partner is not evaluating the deal as a prospective loss. The question to them is how much upside potential is there? If a joint venture is the route, propose a joint business plan. Put forth a preliminary critical path which is aggressive and endorsed by the top on both sides. This will help contend with their tendencies to make laborious plans. Structure an independent board for the new operation for the same reason. Stress the importance of the joint venture's independence to avoid getting ensnared with the insanity of their corporate organization.

If you need additional capital, do the advance work of securing alternatives for a financing partner. You can always present the alternative for the prospective partner's participation in providing capital, but remember this can elicit risk avoidance. There is time later to raise the question before the deal closes. Usually, the later the better. With time the prospective partner may build enthusiasm for the project and want in.

Scenario 3

Your partnership has been underway for 13 months and you are concerned. Production is substantially below forecast and logistical snags are creating tensions. Your sales force is begging for performance so as not to suffer a backlash from customers. The cost to do business is 20 percent above forecast. You have begun to wonder why you got into this deal. It is your project. You are the vice-president for one of the owners, and you are responsible to your organization for the partnership.

You decide to visit the partnership and here is what you learn. From top to bottom, everyone is fighting fires. The start-up issues are behind the partnership, but interference from the owners—

including your organization—is absorbing time and energy. People are hopping from one thing to the next. Customer requirements are not always as important as staff requests from the owners. Some very important customer needs have already fallen through the cracks. Communication is messy. Conflict is frequent and rarely resolved. Something else just happens in another business that distracts. There are no clear priorities and hardly anyone takes responsibility. Faultfinding and blaming are rampant. The joint venture is underbound.

What can you do based on the boundary assessment? This assessment indicates an underbound organization. It needs structure and direction and a top-to-bottom dialogue. Call an emergency owner meeting. Determine what needs to be done to eliminate interference from the owners and what internal mechanisms the joint venture needs to make things happen. Set up gatekeepers on the owner staffs and monitor compliance.

Bring together a cross-section of the joint venture—top to bottom. Announce that there will be no recriminations, but there will be change. The objective is to get things running as they should; the discussion will be about getting this done. You may or may not want to give advance knowledge to the joint venture leadership. Mostly, those meetings devolve into complaints about owners and people they inherited rather than chose. Putting leadership into the group actually motivates leadership to get on the ball.

The following are operator mechanisms often overlooked in the formation of agreements for joint ventures or which get ignored by operators: conflict resolution, development of business plans, customer sales service, and routine communication. Demand that these be implemented immediately. Share some options so the operator does not have to start from scratch in the design of his solution. Monitor progress frequently until there is a turnaround. Assign an owner sponsor to a senior executive in the joint venture to visit with customers. These visits are to confess what has happened and, if necessary, compensate, petition for continued patronage, and establish a fail-safe complaint device for the interim period of adjustment. It is elective to have sales staff participate. Usually, it is better to have them be a subject of the discussion.

Assessing boundaries can provide an understanding of where to begin, with whom, and for what terms or conditions. Boundary assessments elevate the human interaction to a higher level of precision in planning and executing partnerships. Even if the assessments are initially wrong, they foment the dialogue on the issues most likely to affect value on a continuing basis. Physical plant, technology, and financial engineering enable doing business. They are not the act of doing business. This is a human process, albeit machines and money can accelerate the speed and complexity of human interaction.

A landscape is a business intelligence tool. It positions a firm within all probable contexts where value could change. A business landscape portrays value-adding opportunities internal and external to a firm against the backdrop of two markets. One is the market for the firm's product or service. The other is the market for capital from which all firms and governments compete for funding of operations or growth.

THE BUSINESS LANDSCAPE

The business landscape must place the human landscape into focus with the other elements of the landscape: investor relations, all dimensions of the value chain, financial engineering, strategic direction and growth ambitions, the infrastructure for action (structure,

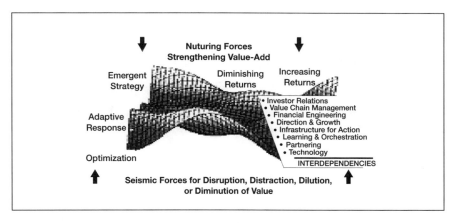

Figure 5-3. Complexity landscape model for business.

learning, communication, and orchestration), partnering experience and philosophy, and technology. This dynamic model of business provides precise analytics of a firm's movements in value.

A business landscape reveals how chaos affects value. Globalization and advancing technology heighten the intensity and overlap among competitive forces and market influences. The capabilities to see, predict, and test assumptions are competitive advantages in the complexity which results. The business landscape provides the means to capture waves of opportunity or emerge with your own pattern for success.

The Elements of the Landscape

Investor Relations

The elements of the landscape are interactive. Each has a special role in revealing opportunity. First is investor relations, which evolved as a business dynamic as corporations displaced entrepreneurial ownership. It includes private ownership, the simplest form of ownership possible. The larger the system or more diverse its pursuits, the less simple the system is. Among individual- or family-dominated firms, the very best share characteristics. The investment strategies of The Cargills, S.C. Johnson, and Mars Candies evidence a strategic intent to build net worth. These firms are not flawless in all endeavors. They have sustained and built wealth across generations when other dynastic families have not. They manage investments to value-add. Their bias is growth for improving net worth. Apparently, their generous performance satisfies the lifestyle needs of family members. The focus then is to deploy returns in capital projects rather than consume them. This provides expansion of a solid base.

Even these large firms must attend to the capital market, revealing information and petitioning sources of capital for desirable terms. Few enterprises of any merit can stand alone today. In addition to their own funds, they entice bankers to loan money to their projects and at times invite other investors to partner in joint ventures. This is their investor relations agenda: internal decisions, debt structure, and, when appropriate to strategy, partnering.

Public companies are another level of complexity. More regulation protects the investment community from abuse. Standards exist for reporting accounting results to investors and exchanges, tax authorities, and other regulators. In the public company, a board represents ownership and has a set of relations, each with its own complications. The board interfaces among itself and with key investing institutions, banks, and senior management. Investor relations includes analysts for the industry which monitor performance across players. Investor relations normally includes bankers and professional accounting and law firms who have intimate involvement with the firm. This array of professional firms may also include consulting firms and advertising firms.

The world of investor relations has been in turmoil and transition for more than a decade. Turbulence is found among issues such as 1) electronic securities sales and purchases, which minimize the role of brokers and bring closer involvement of shareowners to the firm's investor relations, 2) the amalgamation of shareowners more and more into mutual funds, 3) institutional investors possessing such great wealth they no longer can trade rapidly among each other, but simply swap places when trades are made, thus holding a position rather than taking quick profits, 4) the creativity in financial derivatives which compounds and confounds risk management, and 5) the growing influence of institutional investors to promote social responsibility in the firms where they hold significant positions.

The converse, the aversion to liability shown by not taking too active a position on boards or giving instructions to directors, is also true. These issues serve to dilute the concept of ownership in the entrepreneurial sense. That is, fear of liability defeats responsible owner behavior. This fear eschews behaviors such as intimate involvement and imprinting on the firm a responsibility for performance over risk avoidance.

The dance among board directors is more closed than open. Those who guide investors, investment bankers, and financial advisors look for known track records and people of industry networks. Industries function with inner circles in which almost all of the key players know one another. Globalization has expanded numbers by overlapping influences among regions. Still it is a circle of elites. Penetration is difficult and acceptance is a protracted process.

Partnerships are often created among these circles. Still other partnering is stymied because a proposed partner does not meet the test of network membership or sponsorship. Capitalism is not egalitarian. This closed system of relationships at the top is why true innovation often comes from the outside. It also explains why new entrants are smart to ally with, or bring to their leadership, a member of the old gang.

War Story

Uncle Sam's Less than Merry-Go-Round

We had the opportunity to see a closed system in action in attending war games sponsored by the Department of Defense. The department designed these games to signal the end of the Cold War largesse to military contractors and promote a transformation of the defense industry to competitive practice. Uncle Sam's intent was to drain the trough.

What was clear to us was that, in reality, everyone inside the industry was in a conscious and unconscious collusion to keep things just as they were. Little energy went into broad-based adaptation to the new reality. However, four activities did get attention.

First was lip service. A new language evolved leaving people to believe change was likely. The language was pervasive, but the behaviors did not change.

The second most frequent activity was the fight to secure one's past share of business under the old reality by capturing the business of others.

Third was the pursuit of minor change aimed to produce some cost improvement. When whole-scale change naturally emerged from cost containment, the effort shut down or encountered stiff resistance. Examples are activities-based costing or the use of value-added models to appraise projects. Most military and, for that matter, government projects are based on activities within a budget and schedule. Almost anything can be justified. The value system does not use a value analogous to shareholder value-add (SVA). As a result, taxpayers do not always get what they need.

The fourth activity noted was fascinating because the phenomenon ranged across roles in the industry. Everyone was in the same bed, even natural rivals and competitors. The military, as customer, protected favorite programs or ones they failed to monitor on the behalf of taxpayers. Suppliers quickly aligned themselves to the military's self-justification. No longer were these the needs of military branches but the requirements of the warriors, or war makers. The military used these labels to inspire a cooperative response on behalf of the troops in the trenches.

However, there were no wars. It was interesting language for an industry that put forth its role as defender of peace. We speculated what the reaction of the taxpayer would be to hearing how their money was to be spent on the self-propagating, Cold War-like military and seeing the perquisites (driver, cars, etc.) continue, which clearly were expected because they existed for so long that they were routine, only to be noticed were they ever taken away.

Most surprising, the industry analysts joined the collusion. Instead of holding up the mirror of reality, they encouraged the gamesmanship. It came as no surprise to observe the fee-taking prominent in the consolidation of defense firms in the last several years. Analysts belong to investment banking, and these institutions prepared to consolidate another industry.

Taxpayers and shareowners subsidized the process. Consolidation was most likely inevitable, but alternatives could have been less severe. The consolidation drained civilian application of technologies of research and development funds instead of sponsoring them; these could have created new businesses and absorbed headcount in new profit centers in place of layoffs. The government continued to fund the buildup of traditional weapons despite the decline in need. Powerful generals and admirals, retaining their status and power and jealously focusing on their own outdated programs, frustrated the new military. Worse yet, unnecessary overheads continued. For example, generals, admirals, belt-way bandits, and industry executives adorned themselves with drivers and other staff. It was as though a World War II Hollywood director or a satirist of the Cold War had cast their importance.

Our point in mentioning this is not to retell the basis for the costly toilet seats and hammers in defense contracts. It is to illustrate how, over time, an essential supplier-customer dynamic begins to grow in bureaucracy and ultimately becomes self-serving. Within this self-service, all roles are embroiled. The members of the system begin to serve themselves and not their market mission. At least, this is true if owners or end users—in this case, taxpayers—do not fix the problem. Active ownership is a powerful tool for ending bureaucratic dysfunction. So are smart consumers.

Later in the discussion of orchestration, we suggest ways for stake-holders like consumers, taxpayers, and shareowners to assert more influence. Only this will restore entrepreneurism.

Value Chain

Figure 5-4 shows a value chain. It tracks the numerous interfaces and business practices necessary to chart the course of a product or service from beginning to end. One significant matter of importance today is optimization using information technology. Management can reduce infrastructure and establish useful databases to guide work-flow decision making and product innovation. For more than a decade smoother operations based on information technology have been promised. The technology is easily applied, but the human touch is missing, often impaired by poor attention to acceptance and orchestration practices.

Inappropriate application of information technology suffers from two extremes: overinvolvement and underinvolvement. Overinvolve-ment occurs when a firm does not need to replicate its old practices. The best solution then is to impose a "canned" package which satis-fies requirements but does not attempt to address every convenience of users. This avoids costly design, unneeded encumbrance to the sys-tem caused by design, and infighting about which way is "right." Underinvolvement is most apparent in limited training and poor design and placement of implementation equipment. People typically prefer more control over how they will do their task, not what the strategic assignment is. The interest is in doing the job well.

Another important issue in the value chain is collaboration across functions for innovation. Marketing/sales, technology, manufactur-ing/service, and logistics should work closely with customers to deter-mine new products and services. Customer intimacy is a cornerstone to this dynamic.

Financial Engineering

Financial engineering entails capital development and capital use strategies. Innovative financial instruments come to everyone's mind, with special trepidation for financial derivatives. In truth, these deriva-tives are not new, just newly enhanced. For every great loser in a deriva-tive, there is a winner. Overexcitement and greed make derivatives too

(text continued on page 138)

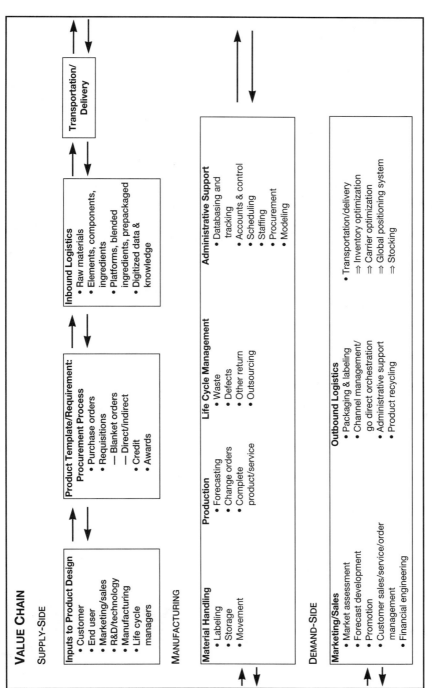

Figure 5-4. A value chain.

easy and open to exploitation. A few bad experiences chase away risk management strategies which could improve value-add performance, offer new means to secure markets, or provide cash for projects.

On another financial engineering front, management is aligning accounts and controls to enterprise units. This facilitates linking shareholder value-add to rewards. Efforts in this regard are prominent in structuring global product units. Most often, companies form enterprise units across the value chain. It is not unusual for these to evolve to include joint ventures.

Partners may be players on the value chain or provide additional sources of investment funds as financial partners. Financial partners augment treasury funds from the individual partners; they may be active or passive. The financial partners may assist in strategy development or operations. Joint ventures (or enterprise units themselves) are then not as likely to be strapped for cash in pursuing growth opportunities or improvements.

These financial engineering strategies do have ramifications for old norms of managing businesses. Firms must truly delegate authority to enterprise units or their alliances. Further, the former middle managers or executives of multinationals must learn the networks and competencies in deal making heretofore reserved for their senior managers. Companies will need training and transfer of contacts. To effect such a major departure from past norms, a company will likely need a proactive plan to realize the change.

Strategic Direction and Growth

The fourth element of the landscape is strategic direction and growth. This can be a function of understanding the landscape, then making a choice in how to seek value. Once established, this element needs to be monitored and, when appropriate, adapted. At some point, a new strategy may emerge and change the thrust to the market. In the beginning, the strategic direction and growth element represents all information about what the business has done to this point and what it knows about customers, markets, and competition. The element postulates possibilities where the company may obtain value. Traditionally, corporate planning groups and the planning cycle have produced this information. At times, consulting firms may contribute benchmarks or assessments. The trend is toward broad, meaningful involvement of all stakeholders. Here is an illustration of meaningful involvement.

War Story

We Do Better as a Tribe

In a privately held firm exploring routes to an initial public offering, we facilitated a comprehensive planning session. Participants included all major shareowners, bankers, prospective investment bankers, senior management, union leadership, and a cross-section of employees.

We used a plenary session to consolidate analytics discussions across these various roles and within some groups. The result was a rethinking of the business, not just as a manufacturer of an auto part but the entire system of parts into which their current product fit. This extended services in engineering design and fostered a strategy for earning a preferred provider status for more than one major auto maker. Management credited the high involvement with reaching a new understanding of what was possible and securing broad-based ownership for results. A few years later, all groups enjoyed a successful public offering.

Infrastructure for Action

The infrastructure elements include all aspects of supporting a business—internal and external—in terms of organization, facilities, and equipment. Myriad possibilities exist across businesses. Most firms, however, tend to structure the operations and support services for partnerships the same way. Infrastructure can be enhanced by sharing resources, outsourcing, conversion, shared facility operation, and leasing. The infrastructure should leverage what is already there. Management must be careful so that using what is there does not restrict value creation. The mission should be to design an infrastructure which best suits the business. To the extent current infrastructure applies, use it. Otherwise, do not impose it on the new venture.

An organizational studies research center asked us recently to examine a food company client. The client merged two large entities, each with its own product lines and infrastructure. The parent insisted that the new company achieve synergy. Resistance to the merger was strong. Our suggestion was to create a value chain services unit and merge services staff from product lines only to the extent needed for the new services unit. The new services unit would use the old system wherever possible but would do what was right for the future above accommodation for the old way. It is easier for people to accept a clean slate and begin again. Retooling bits and pieces of an organization invites defensiveness. When merging two organizations by retooling, the defensiveness devolves into turf battles.

We used this ploy successfully elsewhere for a corporate headquarters services group and a customer sales service unit to give a clean slate for getting on with the future. This provided maximum leverage in both cases for existing talent and assets. In time, the energy moves to the customer requirements for products and away from introspective mechanics and disputes. The infrastructure services unit serves product groups well because that is how they accrue value. Value-added income determines their bonuses. In this manner, loyalty aligns with value rather than function. Internal partnerships look more like real partnerships because of the enterprise unit structures for both product lines and the infrastructure. Picking and choosing among product lines to play favorites no longer makes sense; each is a valued customer with performance requirements for income and continuing business.

For a partnership, it is easier to build a new house together. Any competition for jobs is less likely to be encumbered with old politics. The cooperation is also smarter economics. Retrofitting information technology between two or more entities rarely works and is hardly a means to innovate. Merging means there are winners and losers. Building the new house at least brings an air of fair play and suggests performance really does count most in final decisions.

Partnering Experience

Current partnerships set patterns about how partnering gets done in the future. Not only does current performance need to be tracked on the landscape, but also the manner in which partnerships are done. Prior agreements do not necessarily have to be restrictive for future dealings, but many are because people do not think ahead.

A firm's partnering experience does establish practices and shape expectations for how future partnering will turn out. Prior experience is an important determinant of reputation. Reputation influences others' readiness to join with your firm. Experience is not always positive because mistakes can be repeated. Smart players judge prospective partners not from what they say at the moment. Instead, they form an opinion on what the prospective partner has done in the marketplace over time.

War Story

Tossing Out the Baby with the Bundle

We had a client whose corporate office had given away a lucrative knowledge product as an enhancement to a conventional product facing a market decline. The knowledge product eventually was not only a winner on its own but served to carry the old product. This product did not have to be given away for free in a bundle to be successful.

Not realizing this, the corporate office entered into a long-term agreement with a partner across global regions where the knowledge product was promised to the partner without requiring a royalty or a revenue stream. Greater sharing of the knowledge product income, lengthy renegotiating, and litigation resulted with this partner. In all, this one bad deal delayed progress on the entire product launch strategy, forced the use of partners with less potential, disrupted relationships in the marketplace, and diminished value for a major investment.

Normally, experience makes us wiser for the next scenario. In partnering, knowing what previous partners have done may reveal a challenge of what should be in the future. Lookback discussions can yield important learnings on which new aspirations and expectations for partnerships are set. You may need to articulate and communicate a new philosophy of collaboration to others in the industry. You may need to draft agreements for terms and conditions missed in the past. You may need to orchestrate joint planning processes differently. You may need third-party assistance to help bridge the gaps. Their contribution can be in discovery of differences or exploration of what can be done. You may need third parties to facilitate interactions to keep them on a positive course while avoiding faultfinding. These are key considerations in managing the business landscape for future business relationships.

Technology

Finally, the element of technology shapes the landscape. Included are technologies by which you administer and run your firm, the technology of your product or service, the technology of competitors, the technology of allied industries, and the technology of customers. Small changes can have enormous impacts in technology development. For example, the microprocessor drastically changed word processing, data analysis, communication, and nearly every other aspect of business life. Technology is a complex and constantly evolving business dynamic. Its role on the business landscape is prominent and at times erupts into a new order for value.

Seismic Forces

A business landscape is a topographical display and real-time presentation of a firm. Figure 5-3 illustrates the elements and forces for a landscape. Envision this diagram to be the floor of a canyon with steep walls. The business landscape is the canyon floor. Seismic disturbances can reshape the canyon floor. There is a broad range to their impact. Like an earth tremor, they may distract us from our task, but cause no real damage. The seismic activity may be more like a minor earthquake. Not only is time lost, but manufacturing or service delivery is disrupted. The more severe the quake, the greater the loss. Metaphorically, the canyon floor is eroded by the forces of water, wind, and ice. Dilution to value is constant, and the impact is more severe over time.

In the business case, net worth is lost in addition to suffering the disruption in a productive business. Major catastrophe results in the destruction of value. In the metaphor, this is a major earthquake. The bottom drops out of the canyon, and the canyon walls tumble down. In business, the likely catastrophes are broad-based legal judgments or settlements, bankruptcy, and a sale of assets. These can destroy a firm.

There are many forces negating value which are outside the direct purview of the firm: regulation, competition, crime and war, the erosion of infrastructure, market instability, and disruptive technology. We will amplify each for what is most typical, often misunderstood, or overlooked.

Regulation

The major complexity in regulation is its globalization. Numerous jurisdictions and their regulations overlap. Compliance must satisfy multiple and different agendas. Within common trade areas, uniformity is more likely. It is important to stay aware of trade communities deploying regulations as ad hoc trade barriers. The European Union's adoption of the International Standardization Organization (ISO) standards in quality created a huge bureaucracy and, for a time, served as an entry barrier to Europe for the Americas, Japan, and others.

Competition

Competition too must be seen from a global perspective. There are always more people in more places aspiring to your market share. Competition can often appear not from new entrants to your industry but from allied industries pushing their boundaries. This can be particularly true for products in which nontraditional materials are substituted with an advantage. For example, ceramics and composites are substituting for metals and plastics.

In contending with competition, keep an eye out for intrusion. Countries permit their intelligence resources to delve into commercial and economic analytics. It is not unknown for these to go beyond the realms of integrity and law. The breakup of Eastern European nations and the end of funding for their intelligence apparatus yielded freelance spies. Very capable and now with several years of experience in industrial espionage, these groups are now entrenched in global commerce and use subtle methods. The reports of attacks on businesspeople which horrified us a few years or more ago subsided in the press. Cyber surveillance, informant networks, and other covert means are now popular. The potential backlash for harsher methods makes clients nervous.

Crime and War

Intrusive competitive intelligence is a major motive for crime. A former senior advisor to Mikhail Gorbachev told us a few years ago that the United States is the only country not in the grips of criminal influence or about to succumb to it. We hope this is not the case, but he made his point. Criminality sits at the base of many institutions in foreign lands.

Criminality can be so instilled in institutions that levies supplant bribes and payoffs. A massive payoff defrauds legitimate civil authority rather than having businesses extorted on an individual basis. Crime optimizes. It also gleans increasing returns by setting smart patterns—and thus our third point on cyber crimes. Before continuing to that subject, consider the following perspective on the magnitude of the pattern. As politicians point to declines in street crime, a worrisome pattern of criminal influence is creeping across business like crabgrass.

War Story

From Russia with Vice

A couple of years ago, a business conference for senior executives, financial advisors, money managers, and board directors took place at Oxford. A session on European risk management veered from the published agenda. Participants spent most of the time on one topic—the pervasive nature of crime across societies. It began with the usual telling of war stories about doing business in Russian cities and the arrogance of their mobsters.

The discussion changed in two interesting ways. One is that it reported how criminal organizations moled their ways into major dealings. They may have the labor contract, a services agreement, or a transportation responsibility inherent to a much larger deal. Once present, they pursued growth, not always in a legitimate manner. The other interesting twist was the sum of the whole discussion. Examples given would account for many, many billions of dollars in what appear to be daily business transactions, and they were no longer based in cities or regions typically associated with criminal interests. They were everywhere.

The third point about crime is cyber threats. One of the major findings of the President's Commission on Critical Infrastructure Protection—the group charged to examine terrorism—is startling. U.S. businesses are now on the front line of cyber terrorism. Unlike physical borders which can be protected by police and the military, the insidious nature of cyber threats looms over every modem, personal computer, and server. Penetration can come from anywhere. Cyber terrorists can install criminal acts for detonation at a later date, destroy databases and knowledge storage in a nanosecond, and absorb proprietary customer information without a discernible trace.

The fourth and final point on crime is one dealing with the choice in partners. More and more, the great wealth generated for decades from weapons trading, drugs, and more recently, cyber theft is absorbing legitimate business. This is not a new strategy. It is being done with wealth beyond any prior reckoning. Such occurrences make for Hollywood plots and marvelous war stories.

The sad part is that ownership entanglements and, when discovered, the demise of the firm are distinct possibilities. A loss of reputation, or a major setback, is more typical. This is a time to be very cautious about who you select as a partner or a financial backer. In a world where there are no great enemies, there are zealous nationalists, despots, and thieves.

Wars are more likely to be regional, fought with terrorism, and appear in any region of the world. From skirmishes in southern Mexico with indigenous people to Haiti, Bosnia, and Somalia to the Mid-East, Central Asia, and Cambodia, there is no means to predict them accurately. Economics, nationalism, criminal gangs entwined with political force, corruption of regimes, and ethnocentrism are variables in the formula for war. What is stable today may not be tomorrow or it may be for a long time. Keeping abreast of local developments and adapting are parts of the global business landscape. Not only are events unpredictable, but alliances and obligations among nations for restoring peace are uncertain.

Terrorism ebbs and flows across time. It is more diverse than in previous decades and, for America, a domestic agenda strengthens it. We already mentioned the growing concern of cyber terrorism interacting with physical terrorism. The point to be made here is one of reputation. Our work on multiple continents creates a vantage point for the stupidity of Americans abroad. Here are our insights:

- First and foremost, do not rely on the U.S. State Department. There are good people at State. Unless you have a prior relationship and a strong introduction suggesting usefulness, however, reliable service will be missing most of the time. Professionalism waivers, information is out of sync with reality or out of date, policy will interfere, business information will be shared with cronies, and employees' needs for convenience will impair progress. Sadly, this group is beset by two problems: it is more political than professional, and it is insular, often answering unto itself more than constituents. Association with State is an aversion for deal making abroad.
- Do not break U.S. laws abroad. Pretty much what you cannot do here, you cannot do abroad. You will be sued or indicted when you

return home. Middlemen do not provide the insulation they once did; certainly do not look to foreign affiliates for protection. Consult an attorney experienced in international law. Set aside the coaching of bankers, friends, brokers, and general business attorneys in examining offshore strategies. They are usually guessing.

- Foreign lands, in particular developing economies, are not the places for midlife crisis portrayals of James Bond. Intrigue here will lead to serious trouble. Do not hire mercenaries. Their use will backfire on you. Mercs make good war stories—and the stories get told by your closest friends to people you do not want knowing. We encountered a venture, in which a former Cabinet member was a direct investor, which was employing mercenaries to protect equipment deliveries in the former Soviet Union. A scandal was a split second away at all times. Work instead with local authorities. Build their participation and the need for extraordinary protection will likely evaporate.

- Be cautious about using former senior U.S. government officials to introduce foreign business opportunities. They can get you through the door, but with two limitations. They usually do not have a thorough understanding of local sensitivities, and the doors opened may tie you to unpleasantness related to difficulties with U.S. policy at a later date. The most probable difficulty is entanglements with political controversy because of the acts of the foreigners in the U.S. A bad situation grows severe when the high-profile individual's name surfaces to the media. We know of a case in which a high-profile individual linked a company with a regional government abroad. The company in question was not coached about the regional government officials and their attempts to usurp the influence of dynastic families. The high-profile individual did not appreciate the importance of dynastic families in government decision making. The deal came undone as the families exerted their determining influence. The high-profile individual had not foreseen much; he simply introduced his U.S. client to government types he met while in office. Not only are high-profile individuals often ineffective, they are costly.

Erosion of Infrastructure

The erosion of infrastructure can be the failure to sustain infrastructure or the absence of infrastructure. Regardless, any time your

product or service creation depends on a weak infrastructure, ineffi-
ciencies will occur. In the rush to produce profits, the pursuit of efficiency can become cannibalistic to the firm's well-being. This shows
up when the company does not maintain equipment or keep it current; does not support planning, communication, and training; and
confines work to inadequate facilities.

War Story

Where There Are Big Mac's but No ER

A few years ago, the chairman of a U.S. multinational's hold-
ings in the People's Republic of China (PRC) took us to lunch at
the American Club in Hong Kong. The conversation shifted to
concerns about doing business in the PRC. The conversation then
moved to topics like securing proper sponsorship at both the
regional and central government levels, obtaining permission to
convert PRC renmin to dollars, and hiring employees directly—
putting them "at sea" or at risk without government subsidies.
The primary concern, however, was the absence of medical capability to handle emergency care.

A few days later we were traveling in our sponsor's late-model
Mercedes sedan from Tianjin to Beijing at a speed in excess of
120 mph, weaving in and out of traffic and dodging buses, trac-
tors, cars of all makes, and the occasional pedestrian, cow, and
dog. Our translator explained that our wearing seat belts then
and earlier in the day had insulted the driver's skill. He was
demonstrating how well he could drive.

Reaching Beijing alive, close to midnight, we took pause to
reflect on the chairman's thoughts about what emergency triage
would have been available if a collision had occurred. We
bought the driver a shake and burger at MacDonalds to show
our appreciation and take the opportunity to explain he had
made his point, but, being silly Americans we would not abandon seat belts. Our laws made seat belt wearing a habit. Habit-
forming laws were something he could understand. Over the
past few years, repeat visits to the PRC and inquiries of other
foreigners in the PRC validated the chairman's concern about
medical emergencies.

This is equally true for the logistical system on which raw material handling and delivery of the end product must rely. Some matters of infrastructure are functions of public investment and beyond the direct influence of the firm. All of these constraints do show up, however, on the bottom line.

There is a risk in the inadequacies of infrastructure in other lands. Emerging nations and developing countries are engaging construction of all kinds to enhance infrastructure. It will be many years before they resolve most limitations. What is missing is not always noticed until it is too late. Why? We take so much for granted in developed societies, we do not even think to consider what does and does not exist in other societies.

The risk posed by the absence of infrastructure is more than personal. It can make markets difficult. It also has a bearing on partnering. Take, for example, the difference in performance of two winemaking ventures by foreign firms in the former Soviet Republic of Georgia. As reported in *Business Eastern Europe*, a key weekly report offered by The Economist Intelligence Unit Ltd.,[1] the effectiveness for a web of business alliances turned on infrastructure access (see the inset, "Infrastructure Counts").

Market Instability

Market instability is a seismic force of varying degrees and is widely debated in global economics. Take, for example, the turbulence experienced in Asian markets. There is argument for and against International Monetary Fund (IMF) involvement. Opponents to IMF involvement include those who see no real risk of an economic domino effect for the Asian tigers' troubles to cascade into Japan, then cause further impact on the U.S. economy and other Western nations.

Proponents are those who fear this or point to the comparative benefits of a bailout, using Mexico as a successful example. That country repaid loans and rescued the economy. Notwithstanding perceptions of the economic cascade of Asia's trouble to the rest of the world, the reality is that one region's economic troubles may reach across to another or engender political debate in another region. Regardless of the impact, this is a complexity which is separate from global interdependence.[2] Markets influence each other or other businesses and social dynamics.

Infrastructure Counts

Chalice Wines is a joint venture between Georgian Wines, a consortium of U.S. winemakers Wente Brothers and U.S. venture capitalists, and local winemaker, Sameba. Chalice's export to its key market in Russia is a headache because of transportation difficulties. Railways, highways, and ports are rife with customs officials expecting bribes. Roads are seasonal due to heavy winters, and other routes are not accessible because of political upheavals, wars, and circumstances approaching a state of war. A weak local market is not a viable substitute.

Georgian Wines also participates in a joint venture with Spirits. GWS is a Dutch-Georgian-British joint venture. GWS is backed by Royal Cooyman's, a multinational. The partners made a difference. They successfully export to Russia by rail using a route leveraged through the good connections of the multinational. This venture enjoys other market advantages which further illustrate the comparative advantage in choice of partners and infrastructure access.[1]

Disruptive Technology

Disruptive technologies are innovations which change the whole way in which business is done. The MOS thyrister, the two-sided super chip or microprocessor, makes power electronic building blocks possible, according to the Office of Naval Research and a division of the Harris Corporation (link to http://www.pebb.onr.navy.mil/ for details). If the Navy is successful, then the entire power utility industry may go tilt. AC and DC will be interchangeable, consumers will push back stored energy to the grid, and power controls will be housed in candy boxes instead of huge rooms.

Another example of a disruptive technology is the introduction of integrated customer databases in the airline industry. It took court action to mediate the market advantages of one airline's reservation system. Their broad market linkage to travel agents permitted data-based information not only about their customers but those about their competitors as well. Disruptive technologies outdate or outpace existing means so they may dominate the market.

In the Zone

As indicated in Figure 5-3, the business landscape includes nurturing forces in addition to seismic forces. These can be favorable circumstances for capital deployment, enablers for smooth operation, or receptive consumption markets. What these circumstances will be varies from firm to firm and among the situations they encounter.

The landscape diagram has two axes, together creating six zones. The axes are balanced as continua. One is emergent strategy to adaptive response to optimization. The other is diminishing returns to increasing returns. Cross-referenced, they form a matrix pivotal to interpreting landscapes (see Table 5-1).

Table 5-1
Possibilities in a Business Landscape

	Emergent Strategy	Adaptive Response	Optimization
Diminishing Returns			
Increasing Returns			

As we discussed before, adaptive strategies ride the wave of events coming to the landscape. They invite adaptation. You need close assessment of the landscape to pick the best wave to ride. The wave is a function of a pattern. Your objective is to strengthen the pattern to your benefit. Emerging strategies erupt from the landscape. Emerging strategies mature because you make them happen, having foreseen an opportunity they respond to or create. These strategies are associated with setting patterns and realizing increasing returns. Complexity theorists tell us if we do nothing, patterns will still evolve. They will be random or caused by another firm's intent. Leaving value to these kinds of uncertainty is not prudent business.

Optimization is a process focused on diminishing returns. As mentioned, you optimize diminishing returns to maximize the use of resources and forestall loss. What gets optimized are mechanical systems of production, service, and administration. The objective is to find the critical path which makes the most sense. Here we tend to think of linear processing.

Optimization efforts can have increasing returns strategies in addition to offsetting diminishing returns. For example, optimization efforts encounter human resistance or delay in use. Patterns influencing human acceptance of a technology by users makes or breaks the optimization effort. Setting the correct patterns with communication and training promotes increasing returns for the optimization solution. Adaptation and emerging strategies then join with optimization for a total solution.

As more people understand and feel comfortable with the new technology, their attitude becomes contagious. Their expertise accelerates others' learning, and because of their acceptance of the new technology, others choose to fall in line to fit in. Complaining and moaning are no longer acceptable. A pattern of increasing returns is in place for accepting and using the new technology.

Increasing returns is setting patterns which, when repeated, become dominant. Dominant means they occur frequently and more often than other choices. When increasing returns take place in business, value is created or improved. The value-added takes the form of business growth. Improved value is derived from securing business performance or gaining incremental performance. Improvement may protect value or value-add.

A good example of value creation is Microsoft and its splendid performance. The IBM personal computer (PC) became dominant in U.S. business in the early 1980s. Microsoft was able to ride the tide with its MS-DOS operating system eschewing Apple's operating systems and another DOS vendor. Later, in the 1990s, the Windows operating system brought the ease found in Apple's Macintosh environment to the IBM PC world, and Microsoft's dominance accelerated. So splendid, in fact, is Microsoft's success, it is facing scrutiny by antitrust experts.

In our knowledge-driven world, Microsoft is seen as taking advantage of more than others' complacency. As reported in *The New Yorker,* the Justice Department antitrust specialists began to see knowledge-based markets differently as they understood complexity. They wanted to perceive how markets might be influenced unfairly for consumers or other producers in the highly complex world of information technology.

The debate is over the validity in the premise of increasing returns. Would setting a pattern by introducing a software enhancement aligned with a popular software constitute an unfair advantage? In this case, Microsoft is attempting to align its widely used Windows software with the introduction of its Internet browser software, Internet Explorer. Economists call these increasing returns "network externalities." In plain English, "network externalities" means that the value of a product increases along with the number of other people who are already using it. This is not generally true—few people care how many others are buying the same brand of soap or cornflakes—but it usually applies to high-tech goods for two reasons: they have to be compatible with one another (Betamax videocassette player is of no use these days because it can't play VHS cassettes), and they are often linked to a network, in which case the more people there are on the network, the more valuable the product becomes. (A telephone is worthless if you're the only person who owns one).[3]

Regardless of the position taken in the antitrust dispute for Microsoft, there is general agreement that the rules have changed, in particular, for knowledge-based industries. Complexity has its force in economics, value creation, and value diminution.

A business landscape can be overwhelming. The myriad of interlaced issues within the elements, among the elements, and in response to seismic activity for the landscape constitutes a matrix beyond the capability of humankind and its machines to decipher. We can describe what is happening only at our current level of reckoning. We do know from complexity theorists' models that complexity emerges into patterns. These patterns, and knowledge of how the patterns will move out into the world, are useful in choosing capital projects and managing them. A landscape is valuable if it creates conversations about what is possible or points to forces which require adaptation.

As we mentioned in Chapter 4, complexity can overwhelm and good judgment needs to bring a focus within the maze of possibilities. For this reason, companies depend on the landscape review to determine what variables influence value creation the most, either directly or interactively. Those factors compose the business trellis.

Periodically, firms should revisit the landscape. The trellis can degenerate into a staid planning tool if it blinds the firm to new forces of change. How often is this required? That depends on the situation and the sophistication of the trellis. Quick lookbacks on the landscape should be every three to six months if there is a general feeling the trellis is complete. When to do intensive reviews is a judgment call. Any major change in the market or introduction of new technology clearly warrants an in-depth review. There is no rule of thumb for the impact of changes on commodities versus high technology. Any product or service can become turbulent at any moment. Constant attention offers the value advantage.

REACHING BEYOND OPTIMIZATION TO MANAGING COMPLEXITY

The context for work presents and influences an economic opportunity. Traditionally, we have pursued linear solutions to optimize diminishing resources. Partnering opens the door for increasing returns to emerge from knowledge-based value.

In the industrial era, companies realized economic advantage by optimizing mechanical systems against diminishing returns. The mechanical view carried over into how we dealt with one another. Our relations internal to the firm and how we managed contact with customers, vendors, and the community were treated as processes to be optimized. We managed with hierarchy and control, drawing from bureaucratic institutions like the military and the church as models of organization and authority. They may not be sleek structures for work, but they get a lot of people to move in the same direction.

The industrial age was well suited to these models because the objective then was to forge product from equipment and resources by compelling compliance to linear processes aimed at an end result. This enabled humankind to have more and exploit the resource base. Some marched to a different tune, but basically optimization was the primary aspiration of the modern industrial era. This continues to be true today.

In time humankind learned the hard way, and three forces for change evolved. One of the forces for change is **exploitation.** Optimization was myopic and concentrated only on a product's manufacturing process. Companies took optimization too far. As populations grew and density increased, nature's tolerance for this tunnel-vision exploitation declined. In place of an isolated impact, the collective impact attacked basic life systems. The sustenance within nature—air and water—became at risk of diminishing returns. This exploitation endangered much of natural life as we know it. In the end, the efforts of humankind and nature were at odds. The life cycle began to close in on our existence.

Humankind responded as societies dealt with declines in the quality of life, yet some communities still faced the question of survival. In time, an ecological conscience surfaced and shifted emphasis from resource utilization to strategies within environmental sustainability. Though the ecological awakening is broadly experienced, something is missing. Sadly, developing societies do not always benefit from the mistakes of their more prosperous brothers and sisters. Developing societies continue to take optimization too far, failing to learn how to sustain nature. Nature will eventually force change upon them too.

The second force of change is **learning**. This has at least three elements. First is that "followers" know more than in previous times. Were followers not knowledgeable, they could not create solutions in the knowledge era. The second element is that smart folks do what they think is best and that is not necessarily what those in charge tell them to do. The third point is that smart people self-initiate, and you get more innovation with greater enthusiasm from the people responsible for making it happen—whatever "it" may be: service quality, product innovation, cost-effective production, etc. In the end, smart people need less administration and management. Optimization is less important within knowledge and with those who possess knowledge. They will find a way.

The third force of change is the **frequent** application of optimization. It is so widely applied, optimization no longer distinguishes a company. Everyone is doing it and bringing forth very similar cost savings. The process of optimization—once a competitive advantage—is now a commodity.

Eventually everyone optimized and left no superior position in efficiency which could be conveyed to the customer as a price reduction or value-added for the shareholders' benefit. Price implosion is a frequent outcome of optimization. Markets accustomed to patterns of price reduction continue to demand them. Price wars result and margins decline further, effecting a negative economic reward.

Information technology, fundamental customer sales services, and structured alignment to enterprise units are enhancing optimization. These do promise incremental performance improvements. Big results will be accrued only from adapting and emerging with patterns for increasing returns. This is the twenty-first century view of value creation.

Time-Lapse Photography of a Bridge over Troubled Waters

An illustration bridging the industrial era to the knowledge era shows the transformation in which we live and points to what is ahead. The greatest challenge in building the bridge is describing the knowledge era in a way which is more than clichès and buzzwords. The buzzwords are important to learn for the next millennium, but without a point of reference in the transition from the industrial era to the knowledge era, they are insufficient.

Management consultants, futurists, politicians, and the media bombard society with repeated warnings about three changes: globalization, information technology, and improved accessibility to one another via communication or transportation. They offer little assistance on how to best manage with these changes. The constant echo of these warnings dulls the senses to the importance of their emergence. Groups use the warnings to justify all sorts of programs and investments. For the good of some firms, the purveyors of doom move the firms to action. Unfortunately, programs and investments are often an inadequate response.

Optimization against diminishing returns was the dominant management thrust in the industrial era. This is supplanted in the knowledge era by managing complexity for increasing returns. One dimension of increasing returns is the principle wherein forces surface on a firm's landscape and the firm's choice is to adapt or not. A pattern has been set somewhere which repeats itself. It can happen randomly or as a result of another person's intent. In either case, a pattern emerges because a choice is repeated. The next choice is influenced by the first experience and the initial expectation. With time, momentum carries forward until the pattern is dominant. Increasing returns, the setting of patterns in place, are more an issue in the knowledge era. In the knowledge era, choice is frequent and choice is influenced by the level of understanding achieved by the chooser.

The evolution from one era to the next does not mean that optimization against diminishing returns no longer has a place. The brilliant complexity theorist and economist Brian Arthur of the Santa Fe Institute (SFI) wrote,

Mechanisms of increasing returns exist alongside those of diminishing returns in all industries. But roughly speaking, diminishing returns hold sway in the traditional part of the economy—the processing industries. Modern economies have therefore bifurcated (divided) into two interrelated worlds corresponding to the two types of returns. The two worlds have different economics. They differ in behavior, style, and culture. They call for different management techniques, strategies, and codes of government regulation. They call for different understandings.[4]

Leveraging Knowledge for Increasing Returns

Industries dependent on knowledge are more likely to discover value in increasing returns strategies. These industries include information technology, telecom, biotech, advanced electronics, sophisticated weaponry, aerospace, financial engineering, and commercial intelligence. Any firm's knowledge-based functions are similarly capable of developing increasing returns strategies: design, technology, marketing/sales, finance, trading, treasury, human resources, planning, real estate, law, and tax.

Illustrations of patterns evolving from increasing returns include:

- Establishing alliance relationships creating a "pipeline" through which other deals will be done. (The pattern is the agreement to carry within it additional revenue streams and its flexibility to adapt to future transactions.)
- Cobranding in gasoline retail wherein major brands of quick-serve restaurants are located in service stations. (The pattern is cobranding at a site to leverage the use of the real estate.)
- Developing new technology by placing old and new technology together on a platform. (The pattern is gaining acceptance for platforms as an industry standard.)
- Creating new software or genes which "fit" with old software or genes but which offer improved performance on an additional feature or characteristic. (The pattern is the pairing of the new knowledge with the old as a means for updating or improving.)
- Establishing a gateway technology through which other technologies must pass to be utilized. (The pattern is the control of passage through the gateway.)

- Authoring financial engineering solutions through which levy is reduced on both sides of a border to effect a lower cost of capital. (The pattern is concurrent agreement on terms with multiple nation states.)

Later in his article, Arthur provides guidance as to how optimization and complexity management are fundamental to either traditional processing industries or knowledge-based industries. "Most high-tech companies have both knowledge-based operations and bulk-processing operations. Conversely, manufacturing companies have operations such as logistics, branding, marketing, and distribution which belong largely to the knowledge world,"[5] he explains. This means even traditional industries manufacturing commodities are growing dependent on knowledge and must have strategies for increasing returns. In turn, knowledge-based firms are likely to have optimization needs.

A scenario for a company unfolding from the 1940s to the present illustrates the bridge from the industrial era to the knowledge era. The scenario represents a composite of industries in the United States. Though at different times in the last 50 years or so, they have followed the same pattern of development and crisis.

The American Story

Imagine that you are a producer of a product in the United States at the close of World War II. You learned to respond to the war demand. Now you are concerned, with the end of the war, that you will face a great downturn in business. Your R&D staff modifies your wartime product to satisfy consumer need. Your new market is the returning GIs and Rosie the Rivetors. Their ambitions to start families and get on with life create a new demand. With marketing and advertising to stimulate interest, demand grows. You once again apply to the consumer product your know-how for optimizing production. Accepting a bit of confusion and inefficiency on the front end, you eventually bring order to the start-up chaos.

You are now truly optimizing. You produce a uniform product with a rigid system of controls to manage costs and ensure quality. As time passes, you grasp the fluctuations in inventory by the idiosyncrasies of seasons, regions, and eventually categories of customers. You do not remain stagnant; you begin to innovate. Your workers become more prosperous yet are less satisfied with work in general. Among other things, they lobby for higher wages and better working conditions. Your focus is to respond efficiently to an enormous market demand.

You identify opportunities for components to be made in cheaper labor markets, first in a different part of the country, but eventually overseas. Your overseas "partners" petition you to visit, so they may learn from your wisdom. You are flattered, welcome the visit, and open your doors to their learning. Pretty soon, they are making more than components. You are not concerned. They are selling locally or in lands nearby them in which you see limited or no value. Besides, you are continuing to innovate, and they are lagging behind with your old product lines.

You are more focused on keeping pace with the growth in the boom of the post-war period. There are ups and downs, but in general things are moving upward. Markets in developed nations, having returned from the wartime destruction, capture your attention. The demand proliferates yet again. No great knowledge of customers, logistics, or even technology is required. Other technologies are added for consumption; your technology, however, is stoic. Besides model changes, no new technology is surfacing on the business landscape to disrupt business.

Trade policy is at times disruptive. You persevere and begin to develop as a multinational firm. Throughout this time, you continue to optimize. In fact, with information technology, operations management, and financial models for risk management, you feel confident you can stay ahead of the game.

You are learning to balance the exploitation of resources. You comprehend the opportunity costs of environmental damage and price erosion from oversupply. Sustaining the environment is not yet a popular expression, but supply and demand are economic fundamentals. Too much means less margin.

Then the world begins to unwind. The previously go-go domestic market begins to flatten. Trade barriers and mounting performance difficulties make expansion abroad difficult. Your productivity and quality begin to decline as your workforce grows in its expectations. More than pay alone, they seek costly benefits. Your overhead climbs. Discord among the workforce carries over into views of fair treatment and personal dignity. Better educated and expressing expectations stimulated by media exposure to what others have, employees express anger, resentment, and frustration which stymie work effort.

Energy crises change the basic economics of inflation; price and debt structures change far too quickly and in the wrong directions. You deny the significance until finally the market forces you to confront the reality. You lay off and later reengineer, always trying to stay ahead or maybe just within reach of a global competitor. You complain about outside market forces but do little to comprehend the leverage inherent to them. In addition to traditional competitors, allied industries enter the contest for your customers.

Many of your old overseas suppliers captured global growth markets with or ahead of you. No longer the second-rate producers, they are emerging as players. Worse yet, your financial backers are finding them attractive. Your cost to do business accelerates as you compete for funds. In contrast to your firm's declining effort and product quality, these societies wanting the success you achieved strive for superior performance. Their workers are recently trained, and the technology is not only new but is positioned higher on the learning curve, thanks to what they learned from your experience. Were all of this not enough, material advances, new business services, and application of new information technology reduce product dominance and narrow life cycles. You develop a plan to modernize and begin to value training.

What is clear to you now is that optimizing is not enough to compete. The context in which optimization occurs has changed. The huge post-war market of the U.S. is no longer dominant. The tremendous growth can no longer hide complacency in product development, work force effort, and quality of service—and still other dimensions of customer relations. Trade is opening to provide U.S. firms a gateway to global growth.

Trade policy is a revolving door through which foreign competitors enter domestic markets. Based on the strength of performance in other markets, they enter with cost advantages over certain industries; they even begin to lead creativity as their consumers elsewhere demand innovation. Soon you join them in seeing the world as the market rather than viewing foreign markets as adjuncts to a domestic market.

You, however, have not left optimization behind. You know it is not the whole show. Others will not permit you to abandon optimization. A wave of experts and advisors coach you to make yet one more form of optimization a priority. They tell you to benchmark what others are doing in your industry or assess your value chain with greater precision through the use of information technology. Each is good for incremental improvement. They sell you on their programs with promises of exponential advancement. The bent to optimization continues.

The notion of growth erupts as a dominating influence on your priorities. At first, consolidation and financial engineering are the agenda. In time, these caricatures of growth wind down. The need to let go of the past and attend to the needs of the marketplace is apparent. You search out with customer intimacy strategies what customers want. You learn what will persuade them to follow you to new products and services. Aligning services and technology enhancements to primary products grows in importance. Bundling products and cobranding strengthen the need for partnering beyond the supplier-customer action teams which first encouraged you to partner.

You now pay attention to adaptation. You look among the trends and seek out a way to emerge with the pattern of activities which can become dominant in an industry. This is the pursuit of increasing returns. You aspire to offer the world the "Windows 95" of your industry—something that fits everyone's needs and is compatible with the technology your customer owns. You examine your business landscape and see it as highly interactive with a myriad of forces (concepts, technologies, events, firms, personalities) in the marketplace. They range from community, government, and trade to competitors, partners— who at times may be competitors—and customers.

You understand that adaptation requires great sensitivity to what is happening in the marketplace and the capability to analyze and focus on a course of action. It is much more than benchmarks, because benchmark behavior may be inappropriate to either your culture or current circumstances in the marketplace. This is true because either new forces change requirements or the benchmark behavior impacts and itself alters the nature of the market. The key is to adapt—swiftly and with intent.

As Arthur points out, "Adaptation means watching for the next wave and positioning the company to take advantage of it. Adaptation is what drives increasing returns businesses, not optimization."[6] Acting on his words moves you to the knowledge era. It is a world of optimizing within the context of sustaining vitality—the pursuit of increasing returns. This is complexity.

Interestingly, patterns setting increasing returns are two-edged swords. Patterns may be good or bad for your strategy. They may simply evolve by chance rather than result from intent. Again we advocate that understanding patterns and emerging with your own is the smart move.

The illustration represents a trend for Western industry as it evolved after World War II to today. Gary Hamel, of "core competency" fame, lectured about how a pattern of Japanese dominance unfolded in certain industries. Beginning with the 1950s and the motorcycle industry in the U.S. and United Kingdom, he told the story of how Japanese business and technical people learned from their Western colleagues the intricacies of the business. With a "strategic intent" slowly to secure the dominant role, they began with lesser quality products, learned and adapted to customer demand, and eventually won out.[7] The pattern is repeated for steel, autos, office equipment, consumer electronics, and other industries, continues through to today and their aims are on the process chemical industry and knowledge-based pursuits such as biotechnology, telecom, advanced materials, and information technology.

Having suffered so many industry takeovers and eroded positions in traditional markets, global firms pursue the knowledge advantage in world markets. The advantage lies in a capacity to create new products and services. This requires special talents supplied by solid technical training and gifted student bodies active in sophisticated university research. Again we arrive at the knowledge era.

Dick & Jane vs. "Ivan y Vera"

Mars Candies perceived the wave of political transformation in Russia as a lucrative opportunity. They knew the evolving pattern of consumption would constitute a significant new market, eventually totaling "15M consumers buying at least once a week." Mars' past successful pattern of promoting candy with commercials of "carefree, energetic American good life" did not work in the turmoil-stricken Russia. They redeveloped an advertising campaign based on local culture and turned around performance. Mars was successful in setting a positive pattern in their candy distribution network. It was brilliantly deployed to launch their cat food.

Before going forward, do a lookback analysis. The learning in the illustration from the industrial era to the knowledge era is simple: Watch and manage patterns. In the knowledge era, a firm does not need to play into others' patterns of exploitation. You can set aside established patterns by understanding relationships among market influences and observing their movement together across time. This enables you to emerge with patterns for increasing return—with your intent. A case to illustrate this point is Mars Candies' entry to the Russian market after the demise of the Soviet system (see inset, "Dick & Jane vs. Ivan y Vera").[8]

Consider again our illustration of the composite company and how different things might have been given these scenarios. The strategies could have been initiated or played out earlier by responding to observable patterns. First, our producer takes a longer look at overseas partners. Strategic agreements are struck precluding competition or extracting a premium through rigorous licenses. The agreements address technology transfer fees and broaden partners' participation in rewards—as an incentive for honorable behavior and loyalty. Fees and other returns to the producer from the partnering relationship are reinvested in technology development. Continuous product and service improvement is then a lock-in for partners. They sustain their investment by upgrading their maintenance and operating know-how for improvements.

All this could have begun because the producer observed a pattern for adapting the producers' own understanding of the business. Then the producer could surmise a controlled sharing of benefits. It would have meant a lesser threat. The producer would have gained continuity in value creation.

Another scenario is the producer putting more effort into customer responsiveness—fostering innovation and acceptance by users. Improved competitor intelligence might have further stimulated the need for continuous improvement and innovation. It might also have offset the pattern for decline in the domestic market and the growth abroad.

Still another scenario is employee involvement in business strategy, sponsored with the objective of gaining their acceptance for the business direction. With employees as partners, costs are better contained and innovation is more likely. The pattern of increasing isolation of employees and loss of their interest in work could have been thwarted. Training and investment could have offset the tremendous loss in value sustained in the 1980s' transfers of ownership and reengineering efforts.

Information technology could have had better acceptance, and the transformation of nearly all institutions would then come to a close at the turn of the century. In reality, we are little more than half-way to full use of today's information technology. Still more is available in the short term as telephony, operations process control, and data-based management converge and acceptance for new information systems is too often a generation behind technology available. This is the view if we are honest with ourselves and see corporate life with a trained eye. In a few words, we are not fully optimized because we failed to establish increasing returns when we had the first opportunity.

For Knowledge to Transform into Value, There Is a Shift from "I Think, Therefore I Am" to "We Partner, Therefore We Succeed"

In the knowledge era, human relationships are built for increasing returns. That is, we want to understand naturally occurring patterns or set patterns whereby value can be captured. If a pattern repeats and sets a new order, there is an increased likelihood it will become the standard for an industry. Knowing what is important and emerging with action sets the stage for survival and success in nature or business. Resources are less critical than understanding how to make things happen. Brian Arthur states, "High-tech products—pharmaceuticals, computer hardware and software, aircraft and missiles, telecommunications equipment, bio-engineered drugs, and such—are by definition complicated to design and to deliver to the marketplace. They are heavy on know-how and light on resources." [9]

To achieve adaptation and emerge with innovation, base relationships on growth through learning, understanding, flexibility, cooperation, shared pursuits, and continuous improvement. Presently we are dissolving the old, uniform, and rigid institutions into fluid systems capable of adapting or cutting a channel into the future for our priorities. At the same time, we are condensing the turbulence and chaos, again into a fluid system, whereby the craziness and the constantly changing nature of nature is understood. Interdependencies and organic ways of viewing how life functions in business can be crystal balls for value.

Figure 5-5 represents a conventional organization as a cube of ice because of its rigidity and uniform characteristics. Global competition, on the other hand, is represented as steam. It is random, turbulent, and chaotic. Where steam condenses into water and before it crystallizes into ice, you have complexity. Complexity is represented as water, which is fluid and adaptive to conditions in the marketplace. This is the point where choices about the future are made and patterns are set. An organization has the opportunity to adapt to or emerge into the market for increasing returns. Here is where the real value is created.

Whether in decline or for growth and adaptation, nature's view reveals how things really are. The world is connected, interactive, and unpredictable. Prediction is seldom a linear process. Judgment will serve you better if it is based on a systems view of the events and factors. A systems view integrates the messy and inconclusive along with the straightforward and consistent. Reaching valid judgments is not an easy task. The alternative is to narrow to linear deductions. In economics or biology, converging on the "right" answer may lead you to the wrong conclusion.

Our basic life institutions—school, church or temple, workplace, and community—teach mostly linear thinking. (This is a curious situation given the grandeur and complexity of God's world for believ-

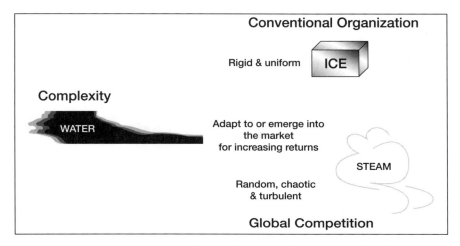

Figure 5-5. Nature of complexity and creation of value.

ers.) The majority of us have been taught the tools and beliefs of this two-points-make-a-line view of the world.

Consider how in business we used to examine performance discrepancy to appreciate the limitation inborn in a linear view. We judged a person by what we saw, not by the influences which may determine the person's choices such as illness, upset at home, the loss of a loved one, a chemical dependency, and so on. Until we dug deeper, we did not know what really caused the choice. With a better understanding of choices, we are able to influence future choices and help the person restore performance. From the business view, the investments to date in training, experience, and rapport with customers or teammates were important investments to be conserved. From the personal point of view, they saved a friend or colleague.

Another example of linear thinking is found in the stock market. We can fool ourselves into believing our predictions and thinking we can make them happen. If we see the market in decline, it will bust. If we see it expanding, our choices will make it expand. We are the market. If we set or join patterns, we increase the probability others will follow. The power inborn to the self-fulfilling prophecy is legendary from the insane Dutch market for tulips hundreds of years ago to Windows 95 a few years back.

In the valuation of assets, accounting practices often report what is on the books and not the market value. Assuming that representation of value is true market value can be a serious mistake in judgment. How many times have firms gotten into financial problems because they believed their own accounting manipulations? Accounting may obscure value or report it when it does not exist. You cannot spend paper profits. A deal based on tax savings is fragile. Why? Reality undoes the cleverest set of books.

In contrast to the cause-effect mentality, nature takes place amidst millions of interlocking and influencing systems. Nonlinear relationships reveal patterns of influence in constant adaptation to one another. In nature, things are sticky and overlap, but there is precision. For example, antibodies in the blood stream are sticky. They grab onto invaders. Despite their sticky nature, they leave alone the molecules which belong in your blood. Incredible precision results in linking only with intruders.

Nonetheless, business has especially embraced linear thinking. It makes for easy understanding. Directions are simpler and there is less complication to master. The comedy is how often we apply linear reasoning in business and get the answer, only to be proven wrong. An example is the fact that most fund managers do not outperform chance. Or we pay taxes to support the purchase of $50 hammers and toilet seats. How much more fun it will be to see more than a straight line.

In an organic or natural view of business, our perception of how to organize and manage relationships shifted from the military and the church to genetic algorithms and amoebas. The latter offer metaphors based on interdependencies and adaptation.

The human thinking process, cognition, for example, is no longer seen as "sense, then think, then act," but as all three activities, often at the same time. This means understanding can be enhanced by exposure to the right external stimuli. You are not solely dependent on your own memory and grasp of a situation. You can take others' ideas in conversation as your own, and if you so choose, build on them or take them to action. This is known as adaptive cognition.

Business needs the capability to be "sticky" and have overlap. In this manner, you achieve flexibility. Flexibility is the ability to work in numerous situations. When boundaries are poorly defined and circumstances constantly changing, as happens in globalization, flexibility offers survival, and with luck, success.

War Stories

No. 1: *The Elves in the Oil Company*

A good illustration of a faulty linear approach is when we worked in a major oil company. The figures reported that the venture was making headway economically. The reality was that staff elsewhere in the organization, not accounted for in the overheads, were providing necessary assistance. Success was largely a function of this extraordinary help. On a linear basis, the venture was a home run. As a stand-alone business, it would have been in bankruptcy. It continued only with a subsidy from another corporate budget.

No. 2: *The Prudent Bad Investment*

Another illustration of misleading linear thinking is a high-potential venture that appeared to be a disaster. The two data points drawing the line were the short-term performance numbers and a read on the management talents of those in charge. The line led to an immediate exit to avoid exposure. In reality, the venture was front-loaded with expenses the sponsor had planned to cover. This was not a bootstrap investment which paid for itself along the way. It was a capital construction project with construction finance terms. Securing the business made good business sense because it yielded high returns and a payback typical for the industry. Sometimes things are not what they seem; other times they are diamonds in the rough.

Look at My Windshield and Call the Weather Bureau— I Predict a Quiet Hurricane Season

When asked why partnering can be so complex, we are often tongue-tied, debating in our heads which of three viewpoints to share first. At the heart of all three is human behavior. Explore the three viewpoints:

- In the grand scheme of things in nature, human life is complex. Partnering is a part of human life.
- Partnering is the intersection of multiple expectations. There is so much going on: trust, career ambitions, learning, and the reality of the marketplace. Again life is complex.
- Focusing and stewarding a business landscape is complicated. No matter how complex life becomes, the best way to manage life is to focus, to keep an eye out for what is emerging, to adapt as best you can, and to keep your focus—unless you have consciously made a decision to change priorities.

To illustrate complexity, the Santa Fe Institute uses a metaphor. They talk about the movement of air caused by the flap from the wings of a butterfly in New Mexico, which sets a pattern. The effect of the air movement cascades across the countryside and eventually results in a hurricane. The point is that, in the sea or air, a movement begets another movement, intensifying as the pattern gains momentum. In the complexity of nature, adaptation builds to a pattern. The pattern becomes dominant. In relativity, the impact is felt with a much different result far away from the source which set the pattern. (Until we learned the metaphor, we had no idea how dead bugs on our windshields in Texas might ultimately affect our hurricane season in the Gulf.)

In our new world order, interlocking influences abound. Economics, politics, social behavior, and health interact among themselves and across boundaries. In this complexity, simply optimizing performance is not enough. As the managing partner for a major accounting firm told us, the work done in an hour today is at the same fee as seven years ago and the firm must do more for it. All the efficiencies have been implemented. Frustration surfaced in his language. He explained that expanding is "whoring ourselves." He insisted growth must be in value-added products and services his clients needed, wanted, or could be convinced to try. The challenge for him is to get clients acting on the trends his firm foresees and wants to make happen. Sometimes this is called "thought leadership," leading a client or customer to new solutions.

In business we spot patterns much like a surfer watches the horizon for a wave. We pick and choose the wave to ride. This is a simple act of adaptation. In business adaptation you take the best of what comes along and ride it out to its logical conclusion. The ability to pick the best opportunity and make things happen separates a good ride from a bad one.

Customer intimacy is a special form of adaptation. It makes clear which wave to ride. The close contact helps you discover what will be the best opportunity. In the same light, the close contact is more likely to draw the talent, energy, and ownership to make things work.

In customer intimacy, you learn value opportunities by getting close enough to be invited into conversations about work the customer knows needs to get done. It means knowing what the customer desires and aspires to. Customer intimacy includes being credible enough to be listened to as you educate customers on what you can do for them.

In customer intimacy, the information float guides adaptation. Details about a product launch or a major capital project can reveal priorities, if not specific new opportunities to pursue. In adaptation, you create value by positioning yourself to ride the wave and staying aboard for the ride. Sometimes it means waiting for the right moment or it is simply luck—just being at the right place at the right time. The ride is a constant challenge, requiring balance, agility, and the smart use of good equipment. In customer intimacy, careful listening, being responsive to customer requests, and leveraging openings to explore opportunities not known to the customer determine your ability to ride the wave.

Different from a surfer and more like a boater entering a placid cove, in business you have the opportunity to emerge from a market and create a wake which, in turn, creates waves of value. You do not necessarily ride the wave but may choose instead to set a pattern on which others will ride the results of your effort. A smart businessperson will determine how to extract a toll for her ride.

Whether through adapting to an oncoming wave or creating your own wave, a pattern is set. The probability is that others will fit into the pattern and repeat it. As more and more people make the pattern happen, there are increasing returns. Whatever the pattern is, good or bad, it will become more dominant. At that point, the pattern creates a new order. This is how value is advanced. This is how value is destroyed.

IN THE FIELD OF COMPLEXITY
DO A LITTLE DANCE

We are just beginning to understand what is known of complexity in life and science. Magazines and other publications are reporting on complexity theory and its application to all aspects of life. An excellent layperson's guide to complexity theory is M. Mitchell Waldrop's *Complexity: The Emerging Science at the Edge of Order and Chaos.* Waldrop's book traces the origins of the Santa Fe Institute (SFI) and the evolution of complexity theory by SFI's principals.

More and more executives and theorists agree on certain tenets offering potential for business. Captured below are highlights from Waldrop's book which may guide the management of complexity in business. Remember as you read citations that a firm is a type of system.

Waldrop drew from a conversation among SFI principals to define complexity as "a class of behaviors in which the components of the system never quite lock into place, yet never quite dissolve into turbulence, either."[10] Simply, complexity exists at the edge of chaos—before order fully settles in.

The norms of business, trappings of authority, and structure of firms delude us at times into thinking firms and their alliances are well-ordered, rational entities, yet the craziness boils up within or turbulence laps at the boundary of the firm's landscape. In these moments, the new vocabulary of chaos is useful. Firms are not always in chaos, nor are they always static. At times they are at a point of complexity. Firms parallel nature when they emerge with strategies from this place between frenzy and rigidity. Firms set patterns which create a new order. The order is a function of increasing returns and determines value.

For many casual readers of chaos theory, the most memorable aspect of chaos is fractals. Fractals are the patterns which emerge from the chaos in fields from microbes to economics. In nature, there are "auto catalysts" which explain why all is not random. Nature possesses an "incessant compulsion for self-organization."[11] Fractals are the result. The message for business is that some patterns will evolve regardless of what a firm does. Order of some sort can be expected from this tendency to self-organize.

A key dynamic in complexity is co-evolution. Waldrop captures a dialogue between John Holland and Stuart Kauffman, of SFI, regarding co-evolution: "Organisms in an ecosystem don't just evolve; they co-evolve. Real organisms constantly circle and chase one another in an infinitely complex dance of co-evolution." Holland is credited with observing,

> This dance of co-evolution produces results that aren't chaotic at all. In the natural world it has produced flowers that evolved to be fertilized by bees, and bees that evolved to live off the nec-

tar of flowers. It has produced cheetahs that evolved to chase down gazelles, and gazelles that evolved to escape from cheetahs. It has produced myriad creatures that are exquisitely adapted to each other and to the environment they live in. In the human world, moreover, the dance of co-evolution has produced equally exquisite webs of economic and political dependencies—alliances, rivalries, customer-supplier relationships, and on and on.[12]

Brian Arthur of SFI reflected on co-evolution in a way which is instructive to businesspeople:

> So the question is how you maneuver in a world like that. And the answer is that you want to keep as many options open as possible. You go for viability, something that's workable, rather than what's optimal. A lot of people say to that, "Aren't you then accepting second best?" No, you're not, because optimization isn't well defined anymore. What you're trying to do is maximize robustness, or survivability, in the face of an ill-defined future. And that, in turn, puts a premium on becoming aware of nonlinear relationships and causal pathways as best we can. You observe the world very, very carefully, and you don't expect circumstances to last.[13]

A new intersection is taking place in the world of intellectuals. They are becoming naturalists. The ethological view of nature, the Tavistock understanding of group dynamics, Herb Shepard's grasp of organization life, and Alderfer's boundary concepts have been taught for decades to enhance human relations. Now the physical and economic scientists are joining in valuing the complexity of humankind with organic views. Regardless of the intellectual banner, anyone who sees firms as human processes in nature will understand real value.

The geniuses at SFI are creating a vocabulary willingly subscribed to by people of numerous fields. They are catalysts for exploring complexity principles across a wide range of organizations. We respect them for what they are doing on behalf of firms because it improves the pursuit of value by firms. They are offering a new way to see how the nature of business functions for returns. As we move into the twenty-first century, economics has a greater bearing on a broad range of issues from quality of life to national security. Improving the knowledge base of firms to contend with global competition is an important contribution.

More importantly, the SFI researchers put forth a means for integrating the ambitions for capital projects with the ways of nature. Envisioning a landscape promotes sensitivity to issues of nature which executives might otherwise ignore. The connectionist view encourages adaptation.

War Story

The Value in Adaptation

Ron Haddock, president of Fina, provided a spirited interview for us about strategic business relations. Clearly his proudest illustration was an agreement with BASF to build the world's largest steam cracker on the Texas Gulf Coast. This is a good example of the value in leveraging your human touch, watching the business landscape, and adapting. Both sides of the table exhibited exemplary behavior. Here is what happened.

BASF Corporation in the U.S., the North American Free Trade Agreement (NAFTA) region member, announced the approval of their parent company in Europe, BASF Group, for construction of a major new chemical unit. Fina staff learned of the announcement and determined a joint venture could mutually benefit both companies. They prepared a proposal for collaboration.

They presented the proposal to BASF Corporation, who carefully evaluated it. The parties completed important work to explore intent and build trust-based relationships. Both sides valued the human touch. BASF Corporation decided to return to the board to present the new alternative for partnering with Fina.

This was a bold initiative—challenging one's own project which was already approved for capital. The board agreed to evaluate the alternative and decided on the joint venture.

A September 9, 1997, press release from Fina summarized the advantages to the venture:

During the last six months, BASF and Fina have developed their partnership in competition with their independent projects. The proposed joint venture represents the best solution for both companies for three reasons. First, BASF and Fina achieve mutually beneficial ethylene and propylene production primarily for internal use. Second, both companies derive significant cost advantages from integrating the cracker with Fina's existing refinery. Third, they gain significant economies of scale, which makes this an attractive and efficient investment.

The integration of the cracker into Fina's refinery will provide an opportunity to optimize refinery and cracker feedstocks as well as by-product streams. The partnership will take advantage of BASF's steam cracker operating experience and Fina's expertise in refining and acquiring hydrocarbon feedstocks.

"With its innovative design and the synergies that we derive from the cracker's integration into a refinery network, this project will provide us with significant cost advantages," said Carl A. Jennings, president of BASF Corporation's Chemicals Division. "This investment will be the largest that BASF has ever made outside of Europe, and it is of major importance to our company because it will ensure an economically attractive, long-term product supply and other key precursors for future expansion in the NAFTA region. We are especially delighted to work with such a strong and progressive partner as Fina," he added.

According to Fina, Inc. president and CEO Ron Haddock, building the state-of-the-art steam cracker facility at its Port Arthur Refinery plays a significant role in the company's long-range business plans. "This investment is of strategic importance to Fina because it will increase integration between our refining business and our premiere chemical businesses while supplying raw materials to our world-scale derivative plants, where we produce styrene, polystyrene, polyethylene, and polypropylene."

Haddock noted in the interview with us that the venture is a gateway to future shared opportunity with BASF through potential additional projects. This prospective, future value played an important role in valuing the original joint venture.

This episode proves the value in tracking the business landscape, building effective relations, emerging against established beliefs, and adapting to better opportunity.

REFERENCES

1. "In vino veritas: Foreign investors targeted the wine industry early. Results have been mixed—Georgia: Chalice Wines & GWS," *Business Eastern Europe: A Weekly Report: Business, Finance & Investment,* The Economist Intelligence Unit, 1998, p. 4.

2. "Kill or Cure," *The Economist,* January 10, 1998, p. 13–14.

3. "The Force of an Idea," *The New Yorker,* John Cassidy, January 12, 1998, pp. 32–37. Direct quote is on p. 35.

4. Brian Arthur, "Increasing Returns and the New World of Business," *Harvard Business Review,* July–August, 1996, p. 101.

5. B. Arthur, p. 103.

6. B. Arthur, p. 105.

7. Gary Hamel, lecture to the Society of International Business Fellows Class of 1991, London Business School, April, 1991.

8. "Cocoa Addicts: Slick Western Branding Is No Longer a Guaranteed Sell," *Business Eastern Europe,* The Economist Intelligence Unit, Ltd., 1998.

9. B. Arthur, p. 103.

10. M. Mitchell Waldrop, *Complexity: The Emerging Science at the Edge of Order and Chaos,* Touchstone, 1992, p. 293.

11. M. Waldrop, p. 125.

12. M. Waldrop, p. 259.

13. B. Arthur in M. Waldrop, pp. 333–334.

CHAPTER SIX

Orchestration

UPSIDE

Orchestration is where the rubber meets the road in building a partnership. Brokers make money from the closing of a deal. If one of the parties goes fishing after the deal, as can happen in partnering involving acquisitions, that party may make money too. Usually stakeholders do not make money until the venture, whatever it is or however it is constituted, creates value. The outcomes for orchestration create revenues and make earnings possible. Orchestration is critical to success.

The excitement in orchestration is the wave of adaptation that can splash onto a business landscape. The challenge—to adapt to an opportunity, to resist being overwhelmed, or to prevent your strategy from being overshadowed—can be fierce. Good anticipation of forces requiring adaptation can facilitate orchestration. Flexibility to respond further enhances orchestration. The key to orchestration is emerging with your strategy and making it dominant, regardless of any interference.

In adaptation, orchestration influences your capability to exploit adaptive forces to serve your own ends. Dancing on your feet is an art, and it can add value. What you must do is foresee and be ready to act on the evolving advantage. Others may see it, but not act. Full and complete orchestration includes the capacity to turn a trend or an unanticipated event to your advantage.

War Story

The Global Cooperative

A good case illustration is the Saskatchewan Wheat Pool (SWP). SWP is the 54th largest corporation in Canada and the largest of the three western wheat pools. With sales over $4 billion (Canadian), SWP is a major force in agribusiness.

SWP is an aggressive player in its industry, with aspirations to be a twenty-first century leader. Both its adaptation and emerging strategies exemplify its approach. As deregulation invited change, SWP has responded in several ways. One is cost-efficiency efforts across its diverse businesses. Another is SWP's decision to consolidate across the prairies, acquiring businesses in other provinces in addition to its traditional marketplace. Technology, is another example. SWP foresaw the aerospace technologies of global positioning and satellite sensing as important resources for the new agribusiness method, precision farming. The company could easily have ignored the wave of adaptation coming from aerospace as did many other players in agribusiness. Instead, it added satellite sensing services to its portfolio.

Of greater importance to SWP are the emerging strategies for growth. SWP, in addition to consolidating, is investing through its Project Horizon in innovative farm service centers. SWP, as a cooperative, launched a favorable public offering of a Class B stock on the Toronto Stock Exchange. This insightful financial engineering is fueling the domestic growth noted and global expansion through partnerships in the U.S., Poland, Mexico, and elsewhere in the world. Setting the balance between the domestic agenda and new global ambition is a key task. In all, these emergent strategies fit with our notion of what business acumen will be in the twenty-first century:

- Grasping the business landscape and the impinging forces for adaptation
- Managing complexity for optimization and growth
- Leveraging strategic business relations in optimization and growth.

Making bold and determined moves for value is a continuous process. Taking the breakaway position gets the ball rolling. Accomplishments to date are soon history. The future is the successful extension of the innovation process. For example, SWP will be challenged to maintain a domestic momentum and capture foreign growth aggressively. To realize these ambitions, the aggressive forward force cannot pause too long or wind down into complacency. Building processes for continuous improvement and innovation fuels progress.

DOWNSIDE

Many great partnerships are conceived and explored without results. Closing deals, making them work, and extracting value elude the best of businesspeople. Pessimism often dominates anticipation of partnerships. In interviews with executives, we asked if they prefer to do business in an alliance or as a single entity. Most cautioned against the use of a partnership to do business. They prefer direct control. They counsel ownership of at least 50 percent of a firm. Were there another way, they would avoid any form of partnering.

Why avoid partnering? It is more difficult to make work than a single entity. So why do these same executives continue to partner? There is no other way to capture the value. Someone else may own a talent, technology, or asset essential to success. The smartest or only way to gain access is to partner. Or someone else may possess the wherewithal to finance the venture.

FIVE MAJOR SETTINGS FOR PARTNERING

Richard Pattarozzi, president of Shell Deepwater, began our interview with an important challenge: deal with the ambiguities in terminology. His remarks focused on the supply chain but have validity in all aspects of partnering. Everything is called an alliance. "Alliance" should not mean there is only a supplier relationship. "Alliance" should indicate when the relationship built on trust adds value, that is, where sharing intimate knowledge will reveal important opportunity and value-add. Pattarozzi's objective is to reduce cycle time and reduce cost *with* suppliers, not at their expense.

We are frustrated by the ambiguity that obscures the value in learnings. It is not clear what someone else's experience means in examining surveys of practitioners or comparing metrics. For this reason, we define major settings within the venues of strategic business relations.

In the chapter on orchestration, we distinguish among the five major settings for business partnering: **shared ownership** (such as partnering among individuals found in legal partnerships including more than one individual and between individuals and institutions such as limited liability corporations [LLCs], partnerships [LLPs], or joint ventures [JVs]), **value chain partnering** (including supplier-customer action teams [SCATs]), **customer intimacy, employee partnerships,** and **passive investor relations.** In every case, the term "partner" or "partnership" is frequently used and refers to the joint human relationships in pursuit of a common business interest.

Figure 6-1 identifies the venues for strategic business relationships. "Strategic business relationship (SBR)" describes all partnering dynamics. A colleague of ours, Dr. Joe Vogel, coined the phrase. Hereafter, we use SBR to permit us to label characteristics which are common to all business partnering situations. When characteristics are unique, we use the specific label.

BUILDING SUCCESSFUL SBRS

What makes a successful strategic business relationship in many diverse situations? Our work over the years reveals as essentials for success, the statements in Figure 6-2.

The size and scope of the partnership impact success. No guidelines exist as to what is a critical mass given the variety of influences and possibilities for partnership configuration. Likewise, there is no guarantee that size ensures progress.

The subject matter for partnering influences what the partnership accomplishes. A commodity transaction appears to require less thought or effort in the minds of executives accustomed to large value chain partnerships or joint ventures. This is a popular yet naive view. What heretofore may have been a simple sales transaction can become complex. Today, suppliers may gain opportunity in the complexity of price, delivery, and finance. Eric Skilling at Enron earned a major career accomplishment by demonstrating that a company can manage commodities in a manner to differentiate value and bundle services. His organization introduced customized supply contracts in natural gas. Customers are able to tailor volume, terms, time, and price indices to suit their needs best.[1]

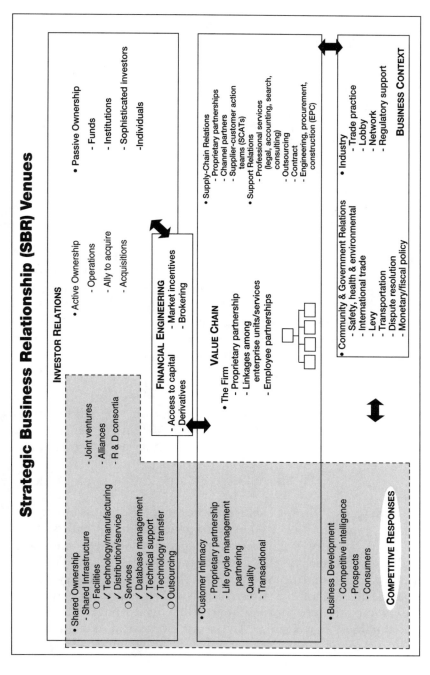

Figure 6-1. Venues of strategic business relationships (SBRs).

- A shared business objective validated by both a market for consuming products/services and investor interest in financing.
- Agreement on terms and conditions for operations and exit.
- Civility in the relationship as demonstrated by mutual respect, trust, and a bias to restore harmony (often called "chemistry").
- Teamwork in the pursuit of shared purpose . . . capability to marry different cultures.
- Sufficient investment to create the infrastructure/system of business (even if elements are shared with parents).
- Respect for any business unit as an entity—its own pursuit (an extension of the parents but distinct in destiny).
- Sponsorship for the relationship in formation, start-up, dispute resolution, and reinvestment.
- Metrics and the means for reward and recognition.
- Fun, celebration, and achievement . . . getting together is not enough in itself to motivate for high performance—the venture must be rewarding and fulfilling for stakeholders, in particular, those closest to the work being done.

Figure 6-2. Essentials of successful SBRs.

Additional success factors vary by their business setting, but the partnering process and the amount of work for the five major settings share some characteristics. There are important differences affecting workload, the issues and style for planning, and terms and conditions.

Shared Ownership

There are several forms of shared ownership. Definitions are at best ambiguous. Joint ventures (JVs) bring to mind significant efforts, often requiring an operator organization independent of the owners and detailed legal agreements. This is not always the case. Some JVs refer to simple market sharing as we find in the airline industry where routes are shared. Another simpler form is a JV to share infrastructure.

Many companies are forming limited liability corporations (LLCs) or limited liability partnerships. These are popular in marketing supply chain partnering. Small enterprises with sales under $10 million are not uncommon. The objective is typically to bring together technology, talent, cash, or other assets owned by different parties for the purpose of creating a new enterprise. A good example is Southwest Convenience Stores, LLC, which melds the talents of Southwest Convenience Stores and Fina, the oil and petrochemical company.

Value Chain Partnering

Value chain partnering covers a plethora of SBRs. As noted in the discussion of shared ownership, supply chain linkages can be under the control of multiple owners. When cooperation is not held to an overview by shared owners, we think of alliances. Again there are exceptions wherein ownership is shared and the SBR is called an alliance.

Alliances take many forms. They can share a market, an infrastructure, an organization, a technology, or be more limited in focus to indicate a supply chain link such as a preferred provider, a sole source agreement, or a simple right of first refusal. Again the vocabulary is ambiguous.

R&D alliances are normally called research consortia. The cost for invention and innovation is shared across an industry or among industry players, universities, and governments. The objective is to fund a breakthrough from which all parties benefit. Were it not for the concerted efforts of all parties, innovation would be too costly to consider.

Outsourcing is another form of alliance. An embellishment to the sole source agreement, outsourcing eliminates an internal service or step in the process. An outside contractor then takes responsibility for providing the activity. Often these are long-term agreements.

The advantages of outsourcing include sharing liabilities, in particular, environmental risks; having a career focus and training for operators shared among similar operations elsewhere (in place of being the odd fellows within a plant or site); efficiencies from sharing infrastructure and labor costs; and independent capitalization for necessary operations and their improvement or innovation. In outsourcing, you pay only for the service rendered.

Value chain efforts are focused on optimizing against diminishing returns. Incremental improvement is the probable outcome, although the combination of two circumstances can produce impressive results. One of the pair is a long-standing value chain which has devolved into isolated segments and bureaucratic infighting. The other is the introduction of information technology to remedy and speed the process. Still, this is optimization and does not capture growth opportunity created by setting patterns which dominate a market. The elements of a value chain are listed in Figure 6-3.

We were benchmarking for an oil company when we discovered the following alliance. It is a good example of how an alliance can integrate strengths. An independent refiner and gasoline distributor, Holly, was able to access efficiencies in the supply chain. Fina benefited in capturing efficiencies and securing supply for its growth in the region. Different from larger oil companies, Fina offered its partner a tall vertical solution, which included oil exploration and production, refined products, storage, pipelines, and distribution. Most oil companies are establishing enterprise units in a particular segment of the value chain. As a result, compartmentalization sets in and the scope of optimization is then limited to a segment such as exploration and production, refining and manufacturing, pipelines, marketing/sales, or other logistics.

As you examine the value chain elements in Figure 6-3, keep in mind there is little standardization in vocabulary used in value chains because vendors in consulting, software, and information architecture introduce their unique labels in attempts to differentiate among themselves and between generations of their own products.

Research on the value chain is limited by the variety of terms used to describe it. This is unfortunate given there is much to be learned about what works and what does not. We do not advocate standards and uniformity, but business researchers should make an effort to compare terms and their meanings carefully before drawing firm conclusions.

Customer Intimacy

Customer intimacy is the essential partnering dynamic in business. It involves a listening-sharing relationship that helps you understand customer needs and how you can best meet those needs. Shareholder value-add is best served by understanding a customer so well, and possessing close relations so strong, you are not only able to secure business but to increase it by leading customers to new products and services. Customer intimacy leverages a firm's competencies in trust, human communication, transparency in governance, rigorous business analytics, customer responsiveness, and teamwork. The goal is pursuit of shared business objectives.

STRATEGY
- Fit (Vision, Understanding of Vision, Strategic Alignment Process (SAP), SAP+ or Architecture (Structure, Information Systems, Learning Systems, StrategicRelations)
- Planning and Monitoring
- Stewardship
- Joint Business Planning and Sponsorship
- Alignment of Rewards
- Metrics

TRANSACTIONS MANAGEMENT
- Transactions Minimization (Information Gathering, Negotiations, Contracting, Product Movement)
- Transactional Transparency (Costs, Problems and Opportunities for All Value Chain Events)
- Transactional Data Basing
- Order Management
- Forecast Fluctuation
- Customer Sales/Service
- Virtual Linkage (Head Office, Sales, etc.)

CUSTOMER INTIMACY
- Large Account Management
  - Percent of your target customers you have. Could have.
  - How do customers behave? Do they buy all lines? Are thy exclusive to you? Do they pay full price?
  - How long do customers last?
  - Share information with partner Repeated for Supplier Rationalization
  - Follow industry standard (increase part or ingredient availability)
  - Common components/elements/subassembly or blends for manufacture/packaing (pool risk for stockouts)
  - Supplier sales force assists with:
    + Stocking
    + Technical training
    + Promotion
    + Limit unnecessary shipment requests
    + Limit high volume
    + Stop abuse of performance-related advertising allowances
    + Avoid delayed payments; extended dates; back orders; later delivery penalty fees
- Material Requirements Planning (MRP
- Manufacturing Resource Planning (MRPII)
- Supplier Rationalization to Preferred Providers•• Same Detail as Large Account Management Above
- Supplier-Customer Action Teams (SCATs)
- Customer Sales/Service
- Life Cycle Management
- Customer Involvement in Product Development
- Customer/Carrier Optimization
- Customer Evaluation/Alliance: Carriers

PRODUCT DESIGN
- Customization or Design for Manufacturing (software, Hardware or Both)
- Mass Customization
  - Transparent
  - Collaborative

- Adaptive
- Cosmetic
- Standardization (increase part or ingredient availability)
- Design for Localization
- Product Flexibility

CORE OPERATING EFFECTIVENESS
- Work Force Flexibility
- Leadership
- Batch/Continuous
- Product Change Over Time (Frequency often changes per month)
- Date of Last Major Rebuild/Turnaround
- Speed
- Net Output
- Average Crew Services
- Degree of Process Control Integration & CAM
- Breakdown Frequency
- Workforce Knowledge/Skill Base
- Work Flow Effectiveness
- Communication
- Network Management and Harvesting
- Cultural Due Diligence
- Cross Cultural Adaptive Capacity
- Experience Curve
- Right Investments Made to Sustain Operations
- Lower Tolerances
- Set Buffers
- Shorten Cycle Times
- Reduce Stepups

PACKAGING
- Naming
- Advertising & Promotion
- Labeling—Regulatory or Advertising
- Simplification: Reduce Products or Offerings
- Storability
- Serviceability
- Security
- Configurability to Material Handling
- Automated Material Handling (Movement, Inspection, Inventory Control Scans, Security Scans)

MISHAPS
- Defects
- Supply Defects
- Transportation & Storage Defects
- Delays
- Supplier Delays
- Transportation and Storage Delays
- Conflict Resolution and Harmony Restoration
- Dispute Resolution
- Inaccuracies in Sale-Forecasting
- Delays in Resolving Technical Disputes
- Lengthy or Frequent Maintenance
- Cost Estimate Variances (In what direction? At what frequency?)
- Engineering Change Orders
- Production Snags
- Demand Fluctuations
- Stockouts and Stock Not In Location

Figure 6-3. Elements of a value chain.

ISIT
- Architecture
  - Fit with business intent
  - Manageable, cost-effective infrastructure
  - Relational
  - Skill/use support
  - Vendor relations
  - Computer-assisted expert systems
- Security
  - Access
  - Reliability
  - Validity
  - Firewalls
  - Sandboxes
  - Policing
  - Repair/correction
- Intranets
- Web management
- Inventory control and monitoring
- Customer sales database
- Customer database (addressibility and store demographics with SMSA mapping and address books)
- Integrated scheduling systems

MARKETPLACE (PHYSICAL PRODUCT OR SERVICE)/MARKET SPACE (DIGITIZED DATA AND KNOWLEDGE)

OUTSOURCING
- Co-ownership
- Sustaining preeminent capabilities
- Operations only
- Skills and knowledge sharing
- Outplacement of assets or talent
- Risk management: loss of critical skills; develop wrong skills; loss of critical functions/control over suppliers

CHANNEL
- Value-adding services
- Incentives
- Forecasts
- Returns, warranty, and guarantee management
- Quality of service
- Material handling
- Delivery performance (distance to customers = transportation cost + delivery/coordination expense)
- Global positioning delivery support and inventory management
- Storage and responsible care
- Inventory tracking
- Technology development
- Packaging
- Adaptive channels

GROWTH AND OTHER OPPORTUNITY
- Pipeline agreements
- Co-investment
- R&D consortia
- Cultural due diligence for M&A
- Transnational expansion

TERMS AND CONDITIONS FOR LEGAL AGREEMENTS
- Intellectual property
- Joint business planning
- Conflict/dispute resolution
- Exit

- Sponsorship and stewardship

FINANCIAL ENGINEERING
- Credit
- Pricing models (experience curve pricing [supplier costs decrease with product life], price towers)
- Revenue structure (COGS—reserves for damaged/returned goods and discounts or allowances)
- Incentives
- ABC or activities-based costing (value drivers)
- Derivatives
- Collaborative ventures (alliances, JVs, research consortia, other shared ownership, etc.)
- Royalties and commissions
- Capital budget for value chain improvements (physical site, human resources, technology)
- Business worthiness of potential partners/customers
- Risk management

SOVEREIGNTY LEVERAGE
- Levy
- Regulatory
- Intellectual property
- Trade agreement
- Research
- Dispute resolution

MARKET EVENTS
- International conflict
- Financial market disruption
- International disaster
- Local n
- Regional n
- Interregional n
- Competitor play
- Customer play
- Consumer/user trend
- Your play
- Allied industry substitution play
- Disruptive technology
- Partnering play—inclusion
- Partnering play—exclusion
- Public attention

ASPIRATIONS AND OUTCOMES
- JIT delivery
- Low inventory
- Zero defects
- Flexible production
- DFM (design for manufacturing . . . transgenics in food)
- Technical cooperation with suppliers
- Total quality
- Optimal exchange for customer—customer pays only for value they use
- Decrease costs
- Increase speed (delivery, time to introduce new products)
- Increase quality
- Increase flexibility

STAKEHOLDER ACCEPTANCE OF CHANGES
- Understanding
- Preferences
- Salience of changes
- Power to act on changes

Figure 6-3. Elements of a value chain (continued).

Once a firm determines a strategic intent in the marketplace, it defines its customers. The focus on customer expectations and feedback drives performance and planning for the future. Collaboration across the firm is aimed at customer satisfaction: leadership, technology, manufacturing/service operations, logistics/channel, marketing/sales, and finance.

Intimacy describes a relationship defined by a thorough understanding of the customer and superior rapport in interpersonal relations with decision makers (as well as those who shape the customer's view of you). Proactive communication and contact further enhance rapport and ensure timely information. This fosters adapting a customer strategy ahead of the market.

Intimacy is built across time in new relationships or by renewal of a relationship. The latter may be more difficult to achieve if poor performance or indifference to customers was part of the first relationship. For past difficulty to be supplanted with a customer intimacy strategy, you will need to expend more time and resources for success. The typical progression of events for building customer intimacy are:

- Research and planning
- Relationship building
- Customer intimacy implementation and operations
- Special events for dispute resolution, growth, or exit

Each process for customer intimacy development, implementation, operations, and growth is different. You build the most effective customer intimacy strategies on trust, transparency, and civility at all levels of your customer's organization and your firm.

Even when you initiate new business opportunity, the focus remains on the customer. An array of customers requires greater attention to your business landscape since forces requiring adaptation and emerging opportunities may necessitate choices among customer strategies.

Customer intimacy secures existing business by inviting continuous customer sales services; demonstrating responsiveness to customer feedback; introducing life cycle management commitments; inviting customer input to innovate services and products; and sharing public relations with the community, government, or trade agreement organization. Customer intimacy can improve financial performance by optimizing infrastructure in the value chain, levy, and intellectual property/trade agreement positions in partnership.

Customer intimacy transforms commodity services and products into specialty revenue generators by bundling new services or products, infusing financial engineering (credit, derivatives, shared equity), obligating customers to technology development or shared channel investments, and pursuing joint ventures in expanding global markets.

The loss of customer focus happens when a product's specialty dilutes to a commodity or when the focus shifts from customer to self or a crisis. None of the aforementioned justifies the loss of customer focus or the diminished potential—if not a real-time decline—in value performance. Customer intimacy is a complex partnering process and is fragile. Continuous attention is necessary to sustain relations and to remain informed about customer views.

Employee Partnerships

Much has been said and written about employee partnering over the last 30 years. Various labels reflect a particular experience or differentiate among consulting products. In the early days, the term of favor was "organization development." Later that would be abandoned from overuse and because it harkened back to too many efforts failing to produce results. With claims the entire organization would change and create a new order of business, early efforts met more often with failure than success. In addition, organization development was linked to group dynamics and interpersonal learnings many mainstream businesspeople perceived as outlandish. The term of favor became "quality of work" or "quality of work life." Companies aimed projects at improving productivity and life at work. Popular among union-management cooperative endeavors, few efforts produced financial results.

Disputes over the color of trash cans and other great dilemmas of the workplace diverted attention from real issues. Deming and Juran, interestingly, introduced a close label yet a different agenda. "Quality circles" and the "total quality" movement were more successful at reaching a work team's efforts to plan and measure contribution. Deming brought back from Japan his quality concepts based on operations research optimization and old-fashioned teamwork. Since it was very successful in application to a hierarchical culture and the clean slate World War II devastation made of Japanese business, executives heralded the quality movement as the answer.

Organization design reinforced or supplanted these efforts by taking a more holistic approach, reminiscent of the early paradigm of organization development. Companies changed the context in which quality teams functioned, thereby giving teams more freedom and rewards for accomplishments. Technology improvement, commercial pursuits, and organizational change co-evolved more frequently.

In an attempt to bring a stronger statement of change, organization design was relabeled as "transformation" or "revitalization" efforts. Indicating longer term initiatives, the objective is creation of a new work culture attuned to "incorporating employees fully into the process of dealing with business challenges," "leading from a different place," and "instilling mental disciplines."[2]

In their article, "Changing the Way We Change," Pascale, Millemann," and Gioja explain, "Done properly, these three interventions will create a landmark shift in an organization's operating state or culture by significantly altering the way people experience their own *power* and *identity* and the way they deal with *conflict* and *learning*."[3]

They observe further, "The problem is that the whole burden of change typically rests on so few people. In other words, the number of people at every level who make committed, imaginative contributions to organizational success is simply too small. More employees need to take a greater interest and a more active role in the business. More of them need to care deeply about success."[4]

In 20 years, we have seen both the partial attempt at change and the roaring success. The difference is startling in business performance and the life worth living at work. Nonetheless, the history of linear, bureaucratic, and control-based models in business is much longer and supported by powerful devotees.

There are two interesting phenomena about employee partnering in an environment generally supportive of SBRs. One is akin to when parents treat their children better in public than in private. There is a concern for the perceptions of others. The second aspect of employee partnering is genuine behavior and more important to value. This is the recognition that those closest to the work influence partnering results. If employees are not aligned to partnering efforts, a company will suffer serious errors.

War Story

Don't Read My Lips Today

In a natural resources company, senior management and the marketing organization followed the lead of a marketing advisor. They created a life cycle management program to bundle services, secure share and premium price, and differentiate their commodity product. Of course, the cornerstone was environmental responsibility.

The CEO conveyed a mixed message to the organization. This new life cycle management—which he had not explained well enough to his direct reports—was not deemed as important as cutting costs. This led to one of his profit centers cutting costs so severely that numerous environmental violations were noted in a regulatory inspection.

To compound the problem, a program involving employees in the business turned down the employee middle management task force recommendation to fix the problem. The violations were repaired, but no one believed environmental responsibility was important to the business unless something was discovered by a regulator. A customer visit to prove that the regulator's concerns had been addressed met with disaster. One of the violations was repeated. This endangered the entire life cycle management program—with this customer and others. Competitors and the customer made the snafu known in the marketplace.

Later management took the employee involvement process more seriously. The effort had to dig itself out of a hole in terms of credibility in the eyes of employees. As expected, the early interference slowed progress and diluted results. On the specific issue of the incidents, some upper managers deny the employee involvement effort helped in the clean up. The subject became one that both sides agree to disagree upon. How much further the effort might have gone with a more honest approach about the controversy!

On the other hand, employee partnering offers significant results:

War Story

A Plant Too Tough to Die

In what we later called the "Fayetteville" model, a plant by this name thwarted closure by achieving extraordinary results in quality, through-put, safety, and cost containment. They also pursued outsourcing, established partnering relations with utility suppliers to reduce the cost of inputs, plus partnered elsewhere in their own firm and with other firms to leverage excess storage space as a multipurpose distribution system—creating additional revenue streams. That was several years ago, and the plant is still in operation. From engineering to operations to maintenance to human resources to lab services and upper management, the commitment was to success.

The model was replicated in a union situation overseas in the Pacific Rim involving a sister unit. It succeeded in a like manner, with a record three days to reach the appropriate labor accord in contrast to the normal six or more months.

Passive Investor Relations

Some argue that there is no partnership between shareowners and the enterprise in which they possess stock. So passive is the ownership that boards and senior managers set the course with little regard for shareholders. Shareholder activism over the last decade and a half has helped to curb this, although the interaction has been more turbulent than productive.

This has begun to change greatly with the successes of firms like Batchelder and Partners of La Jolla. They secure a less-than-majority ownership and pursue relational investment. By relational investment, they mean securing a few board seats. They then establish rapport with other board members and management sufficient to set a more prosperous direction. They do not emphasize control or related turf disputes but rather what needs to be done for enhancing shareholder value. They exercise the owner perogative typical to entrepreneurs; that is, they proactively offer their outsider's view as counsel to management and expect to be taken seriously because it is their and their investors' money at stake.

Selected by the powerful California Public Employees Retirement System (CalPERS), representing $127 billion in retirement monies of California state personnel, Batchelder and Partners manage a $700-million fund for under-performing companies. In a sharp departure from Dave Batchelder's earlier career days as corporate raider T. Boone Pickens' COO, Batchelder and his colleagues, Joel Reed, Kathy Scott, and James Zehentbauer, now do not seek a takeover. They simply obtain a few board positions. In Batchelder and Partners' view, working with management by challenging them to value-add produces superior results with less hassle. They point to the quadrupling of stock value for their intervention at MacFrugal's Bargains-Close-Outs Inc. as proof. There a collaboration with management among significant shareholders effected a turnaround. It is important to note that 1993 changes in SEC rules regarding collaboration by phone or mail among stock owners makes the passive influence process easier.[5]

CalPERS, long an activist fund, has succeeded at a grander scale. They "pushed directors to replace the underperforming leaders of General Motors Corp., Eastman Kodak Co., and International Business Machines Corp."[6] The direct use of board directors is something they do through funds in which they invest.

Do not expect there to be an overabundant application of passive board influence. Despite the success of Batchelder and Partners, fund managers are concerned about risks which may be inherent for activist roles in an investment. These include, according to Doug Willis of the Associated Press, "increased liability exposure, potential conflicts of interest and insider status—which could restrict . . . freedom to trade."[6] It seems traditional operations managers are not the only ones who are risk aversive.

Lost in the millions of shareholders, we have little impact by ourselves. Melding our resources with others in pension funds or mutual funds, we rely on professional money managers to pick board members and assert on our behalf. Passive ownership sheds us of entrepreneurial responsibility. When this happens, we steward our money's use less and react to abuse with an opportunistic sell—when the first opportunity presents itself.

Choosing responsible fund managers creates differentiation among them. Instead of entrusting your money to the guy who went to the right schools but did not learn, was the son of someone but did not get the genes which count for finance, or entered the brokerage business because of the 1980s movies about big-time deal makers, pick passive representatives who ensure that management's choices serve shareholder value-add. This is the bond that counts to make the passive investor come alive in today's superstructures.

Before we will see a partnership between boards and management which truly challenges for shareholder value-add, there must be more worthy partners in the shareholder-to-fund manager-to-board bonds. We, the fund owners, own this selection problem. We, the shareowners, share in this.

IN THE END

Orchestration is complex. There are numerous settings in which partnering takes place. Each has its own agenda for implementation and successful operation. Orchestration is vital to extracting value from a deal for the owner. At the end of the day, owners are responsible for what happens to value along with the people they employ. The partnership between owners and their employees, managers, supervisors, or contributors is the cornerstone to all success. Even a partnership among firms rests on the ability of the individual firms to fulfill commitments and encourage performance. There is no rocket science here, just fair play in hard work against a business intent.

REFERENCES

1. Peter Tufano, "How Financial Information Can Advance Corporate Strategy," *Harvard Business Review,* January-February, 1996, p. 138–139.
2. Richard Pascale, Mark Millemann, Linda Gioja, "Changing the Way We Change," *Harvard Business Review,* November-December, 1997, p. 127–139.
3. R. Pascale, *et al.,* p. 128.
4. R. Pascale, *et al.,* p. 127–128.
5. Seth Lubove, "The King Is Dead, Long Live the King," *Forbes,* July 15, 1996, p. 64.
6. Doug Willis, "Major Pension Fund Downplays Policy on Board Representation," Associated Press, *Houston Chronicle,* Section C, December 27, 1997, p. 2.

Index